"I've known Rob for twenty years, and I've seen him grow and go through some of the most difficult and unfathomable experiences a human being can face. Through it all, Rob has continued to inspire hundreds of thousands all over the world through his personal story and unwavering faith in the One who makes all things work together for our good. I am so glad this book is out there for those who might feel undervalued, overlooked, defeated, and forgotten. God sees you. This book will encourage you."

Tim Byrne, professional skateboarder and pastor

"*Vulnerable* is a word I've heard said when I step off the stage, and the way that Rob lays his whole heart out on these pages for the world to see is exactly that. Thank you for being so real, Rob. I have to keep going, because you are."

Ben Fuller, Christian singer and songwriter

"Rob Roozeboom's book is packed with heartache and humor, but most importantly perseverance. *Broken Still Chosen* powerfully illustrates how we can rise above our greatest difficulties and lean on our faith. It's a testimony to how weakness can show strength and how God uses even broken people."

Adrie Groeneweg, president and founder
of Pizza Ranch, Inc.

"*Broken Still Chosen* is a powerful, inspiring testament to resilience and faith. Rob Roozeboom's candid narrative of navigating life's challenges offers a raw and honest portrayal of facing adversity and finding faith. This book is, at turns, deeply transformative and unexpectedly hilarious. Get yourself a copy of this book from my friend Rob—a gifted storyteller, a beacon of God's grace, and an inspiration to thousands."

Jennifer Dukes Lee, bestselling author of *Growing Slow*,
It's All Under Control, and *Stuff I'd Only Tell God*

T0030632

"Rob has been a faithful partner in the alliance of evangelists for many years, leading the way in encouraging and supporting others in the work of the gospel. He is a friend and kindhearted soul, following the example of our Savior. I thank God for Rob, his passion for the Lord, and his commitment to the gospel. Despite the challenges he has faced in his own life, Rob has lived with a deep care and love for others—giving his life to share the message of hope in Jesus Christ. I'm confident that his story and the lessons within this book will encourage and bless many."

Andrew Palau, evangelist and author

"We've known Rob for a couple decades, and he is one of the most inspiring, persistent, and courageous humans we've ever met. *Broken Still Chosen* is not for perfect people living in a perfect world; it is for the broken people who live in a broken world yet make a courageous choice to rise above the circumstances of life and live an extraordinary life. His wisdom is born through pain and will enrich your life no matter what you are enduring."

The Saylors Brothers (Kenny and Kyle), filmmakers

"I'm so grateful for Rob's willingness to share a part of his own brokenness and battle with muscular dystrophy in *Broken Still Chosen*. I've known Rob for years, but in the book, Rob shares a part of his story that I hadn't heard before. Whatever you're going through or have been through, this book will meet you right where you're at and give you the courage to keep pursuing God's call for your life—just like Rob is doing."

Adam Weber, lead pastor of Embrace Church,
podcast host, author

BROKEN
STILL
CHOSEN

BROKEN STILL CHOSEN

FINDING HOPE IN JESUS WHEN YOU FEEL UNLOVED, UNSEEN, OR FORGOTTEN

ROB ROOZEBOOM

WITH KATHLEEN HAUCK GROOM

Chosen

a division of Baker Publishing Group
Minneapolis, Minnesota

Published by Chosen Books
Minneapolis, Minnesota
ChosenBooks.com

Chosen Books is a division of
Baker Publishing Group, Grand Rapids, Michigan

Printed in the United States of America

Library of Congress Cataloging-in-Publication Data
Names: Roozeboom, Rob, author. | Groom, Kathleen Hauck, author.
Title: Broken still chosen : finding hope in Jesus when you feel unloved, unseen, or
    forgotten / Rob Roozeboom with Kathleen Hauck Groom.
Description: Minneapolis, Minnesota : Chosen Books, a division of Baker Publishing
    Group, [2024] | Includes bibliographical references.
Identifiers: LCCN 2023048312 | ISBN 9780800772765 (paper) | ISBN 9780800772826
    (casebound) | ISBN 9781493446964 (ebook)
Subjects: LCSH: Muscular dystrophy—Religious aspects—Christianity. | Hope—
    Religious aspects—Christianity. | Grief—Religious aspects—Christianity.
Classification: LCC BV4910.6.M87 R66 2024 | DDC 248.8/6196748—dc23/
    eng/20231219
LC record available at https://lccn.loc.gov/2023048312

Cover Design: Micah Kandros Design

Baker Publishing Group publications use paper produced from sustainable forestry practices and postconsumer waste whenever possible.

24 25 26 27 28 29 30   7 6 5 4 3 2 1

Dedicated to my wife, Sharla,
who is my rock—after Jesus!
And to our kids, Jager, Riley, and Aidan,
who have blessed me on this crazy journey
of life together in ways they may never know.

CONTENTS

1

Everyone Is Broken

I sat on the hard tile floor at the doctor's command.

"Stand up."

I stood.

"Sit on the floor."

I sat again.

"Stand up."

I stood, but I didn't like it. Why was the doctor telling me to sit down and stand up over and over again? My nose wrinkled at the way the hospital smelled. I still don't like that clinical smell. At age five, I thought everything around me that day was strange, especially the doctor. I had a hard time understanding him when he talked, and he had a long name I couldn't pronounce, like Dr. Eisenhowski or something like that. He ordered me again, "Sit on the floor."

You sit on the floor! I wanted to shout. *I'm fine! What do you want me to sit on the floor for anyway if you're just going to tell me to stand back up again?* Taking directions from strangers was never my favorite thing, but Dad was sitting there and I didn't want to get in trouble, so I did what the doctor said.

The tile floor felt cold. I looked up at my mom and dad. They were watching the doctor closely as he made his observations.

We had made the trip to the doctor's office because of my older sister, Amy. Instead of her heels hitting the floor when she walked, she pranced around on her tiptoes. My parents were concerned, so they made an appointment for her at the hospital in Iowa City, nearly one hundred miles from our farm.

When they took Amy to the doctor to see why she walked on her tiptoes, they had no idea that balancing on the balls of her feet was a classic symptom of a terrible disease. They discovered that in addition to having tight Achilles tendons, my sister also had muscular dystrophy (MD), "a group of diseases that cause progressive weakness and loss of muscle mass."[1] In all types of muscular dystrophy, abnormal genes, sometimes called mutations, interfere with the production of proteins essential to building healthy muscle. In other words, your muscles deteriorate over time, until normal, independent daily functions you were once able to do become extremely difficult and eventually impossible to do on your own.

My sister's diagnosis came as a shock to my parents. As far as they knew, there had been no history of MD in the family.

But now that MD had been discovered, it was highly possible Amy wasn't the only one in the family with the disease. The doctor told my parents that since one of their children had MD, he figured the rest of us kids had it as well. The rest of us being me and my little brother, Bill. Following the doctor's recommendation, my parents had us all tested.

The visit to the doctor began a process of medical testing and asking lots of questions. Bloodwork showed that my sister had high levels of creatine phosphokinase, or CPK, an enzyme in the skeletal muscles, heart, and brain—and an indicator of muscular dystrophy. I also had high levels of CPK, so the doctor was taking a closer look at me to determine if I had MD like my sister.

After he finished watching me sit and stand multiple times, he observed me as I walked the halls of the hospital. Then he asked me to run. I looked at the doctor to make sure I'd heard him right. *You mean I get to run in the hallways of the hospital? Yes, sir. Let me run right out of here!*

I took off down the hall as fast as I could. Despite my best efforts, I didn't escape. We returned to the examination room for more sitting on the floor or other stupid stuff, I assumed.

"Okay, now we're going to do a little test." The doctor took my left arm, lifted it up, turned it over, and pulled at the skin. Before I knew what he was doing, he chopped off a piece of it. I still have the mark from where he sliced the piece of skin from my upper arm. It stung like a son-of-a-gun. He tested all five of us: my parents and my siblings. We all have the same scars on our arms.

That was the day we discovered I have muscular dystrophy. My little brother, Bill, does not. The official diagnosis was handed down when I was only five years old, but the symptoms didn't show up until several years later.

We learned more about my MD when I was in second grade, even though I wasn't showing any symptoms yet. At that same time, Amy had her Achilles heels lengthened so she could walk with her feet flat on the floor, leaving her with scars on the backs of her legs. I didn't have major surgery like Amy, but I did get my skin cut again. This time we had to go beyond the slicing-off-skin-from-my-arm test. I needed a muscle biopsy.

I had to be put under for the procedure. When I woke up in the hospital bed, I felt something on the side of my left leg. I looked to see the doctor stitching up my leg where he had made the incision. It stung, but I didn't cry. As a reward for not crying, I received a stuffed animal that I named Ralph. Ralph was with me for a long time, both as a comfort and as a reminder that I had taken getting stitched up like a champ.

They sent the muscle biopsy to be tested, and that began the long journey to identify exactly what form of muscular dystrophy

I had. At the time, they thought I had Becker muscular dystrophy, which enlarges the calf muscles and affects the heart, leading to cardiomyopathy. It wasn't until I was an adult that we discovered I had limb-girdle muscular dystrophy—a type of MD that causes weakness and wasting away of the muscles in the arms and legs. Limb-girdle muscular dystrophy targets the muscles that are closest to the body, mainly the shoulders, upper arms, pelvic area, and thighs.

As a little kid I didn't know what any of that meant or what someday my body was going to be able to do, or more specifically *not* be able to do. I had no idea what I was up against. I knew I had a diagnosis of MD, but that didn't really mean much to me at the time. I'm glad I didn't know it then. My ignorance allowed me to just be a kid, at least for a while.

Sometimes Giving It All Isn't Enough

For the first nine years of my life, our family lived on a farm in the middle-of-nowhere Iowa. I loved living on the farm, spending time with Dad, tagging along on the tractor, and playing outside all day long. I dreamed of being a farmer myself someday. But by the time I was in sixth grade, my dad was no longer a farmer; now he was a pastor. I was no longer a farm kid; now I was a city kid trying to live out my second love—sports.

I grew up in the era of Michael Jordan, Magic Johnson, Larry Bird, and so many of the greats from time past. Since we'd left the farm, I had new dreams of playing in the NBA, or even better, my stronger dream of being in the NFL. For sure at least playing college football at a Division 1 school. (I'm literally laughing out loud as an adult writing this. Who was I kidding with my dreams of being a pro athlete?)

I loved watching Michael Jordan, arguably the best or at least one of the best to ever play the game of basketball. Legend had it that he was cut from his high school team his sophomore year, but

Michael never gave up and came back better than ever the next year. And most of us know what happened after that. He played at North Carolina, was the third overall pick in the NBA, and went on to win six NBA Championships, six NBA Finals MVPs, ten scoring titles, and five MVPs. He also played on the Olympic Dream Team and received many other accolades and awards. (It came out later that Michael hadn't actually been cut from the team, but made JV, which was normal for a sophomore.[2] Still, he worked really hard to get where he was.) Michael Jordan showed kids like me that if you work hard and don't quit, you can become great. And I believed it.

At age twelve I was obsessed by the dream of running out of the locker room tunnel on a Friday night past the cheerleaders lined up yelling, "Rob! Rob! Rob!" as I ran by. In my dream, I'd pass them with a flirty look on my face and croon, "How you doin'?" Then, basketball in hand, I'd jog out with my team and leap up toward the basket. I'd act like I dunked it, and all the cheerleaders again would yell, "Rob! Rob! Rob!" My dream to become a star athlete always included cheerleaders.

Rather quickly, however, I realized that making this dream a reality was going to be a bigger fight than I had imagined.

The day we had to run the mile in sixth grade didn't help. In fact, it changed everything.

I'm still not sure why we had to run a mile as twelve-year-olds, but hey, I don't make the rules. The PE teacher had stood in front of our class and made the announcement a few days earlier. "Next time, class, we're going to run the mile. Be prepared."

The day came. I thought about how the gym coach had told us to prepare, so I did. In fact, I had spent the whole morning preparing—praying to God that something would happen to get me out of it. Maybe He could cause a fire or a tornado. Maybe He could give me a fever with severe vomiting. As I sat in class the period before gym, I even prayed that He'd knock one of the ceiling tiles down to land on my head and injure me. But I wasn't so lucky.

At the beginning of PE that day, class began with the gym teacher's pep talk. "Listen up, young people. Today we're going to separate the men from the boys and the women from the girls."

Okay, he might not have said that, but it felt something like that.

He went on. "Here are the rules. We're going to run around the school three times as fast as you can." Underneath his breath I think he was saying, "This will determine whether you're important or not, and whether or not you'll ever play on the varsity team"—finishing off with his evil laugh. Maybe that's all in my head. It was a long time ago. But for sure I know it was a three-lap run around the school. And our school was big. By the time we were done, we would have run a mile.

All of us sixth graders stood at the ready, boys and girls prepared to show the world who's who in this class of world-changers. The winner, or at least those who finished in the top three, would win the Presidential Award and have their name written in the varsity coaches' team roster. I gave myself a pep talk. *Today is a big day. Don't screw it up.*

Standing on the track with everyone starting to line up, I could already feel sweat running down my face. I knew this day would be pivotal in my ever-developing social life. If I didn't do well, the news would surely spread, and by the time seventh period rolled around, everyone would know my plight—friends, teachers, coaches, and (sigh) the cheerleaders.

We lined up like thoroughbreds with steam coming out of our nostrils, ready to set new records. I stood there with my Nikes laced tight and my sweatpants sticking to my skin. *I can do this.*

Our gym coach came over wearing his classic 1980s attire: shiny sweats and a T-shirt. Before I knew it, he had grabbed the whistle around his neck, yelled, "Ready, set, go!" and gave the whistle a short, shrill blow. It was on—no turning back now. Our date with destiny had begun and we were off.

I knew in my heart I wasn't going to win, but I thought at least I could finish somewhere in the middle. I could find a crowd of runners to blend in with so I wouldn't get noticed. I picked a guy in front of me and tried to match his pace step for step. Then I put my head down and willed my feet forward, one sneaker at a time. *I can do this,* I kept telling myself. *I can do this. I must do this!*

The next thing I knew, someone was passing me on my right. I looked up, thinking, *I hope it's not a girl,* and that's when I knew my day was over. The person passing me on my right was not a girl, but the guy who'd been ten steps in front of me when we started. I wasn't being passed . . . I was being lapped! He was only the first in a long line of people to lap me before we'd even hit our third time around the track—boys, girls, short, tall, big, small—I watched them out of the corner of my eye as they came around me, doubling my speed.

No, this can't be happening! The shock of seeing all these kids passing by ripped from my heart what little hope I had, and I realized right then and there . . . I can't do this.

Wanting to get out of this nightmare, I tried to think of a way to make it end. What if I pretended to trip, fell over into the grassy infield, and began yelling, "My hamstring! My hamstring!" Or "My calf! My calf!" I really didn't care which muscle it was; I just wanted this nightmare to be over. But instead I pressed on, and I finished dead last. I'm not sure if everyone else was already back in class by the time I got done, or if it was the next day, but it seemed like forever before I finished.

I gave it all I had, but I didn't finish that mile in any respectable time. I started with the guys and finished with the girls. Behind the girls, actually. I think an old lady with a walker passed me. I didn't earn any points that day toward my dream of becoming a famous athlete coming true. Quite the opposite. I've never been one to quit easily, and I've always had the attitude "I can beat this," but that day caused me to wrestle with my reality. The very real feeling of "My dream may never come true" swept over me. Did I just see my dreams die right in front of me?

Has this ever happened to you? Maybe you are reading this book because your dream feels like it's been forgotten, or worse, you personally feel forgotten and you've lost all hope. Perhaps your dream came crashing to the ground, leaving you convinced you are unloved and unseen. Or maybe you're white-knuckling your dream, like I did, determined to see it through, yet nothing seems to be happening and you're starting to face the possibility it may not come true. My friend, if you are wrestling with the death of a dream, you're not alone. And you're not without hope, even though it might feel like it today. Although a dream may have died, it doesn't mean God isn't raising another one up in you. I've learned to dream new dreams. God has rescued and inspired me in so many undeniable ways. He wants to do the same for you.

We Can't Fix Our Brokenness on Our Own

For the longest time I thought I was the only one broken, and I felt literally broken. My body wouldn't do what a "normal" kid's body would. I believed if I just tried harder, I could fix it. *If I just will it, I can beat it! Then I won't be broken. I can be like everyone else. I won't stand out so much.*

As I entered into high school, my heart ached to fit in. My parents could see how badly I was hurting. In their attempt to help, they sent me to a Christian weekend with other teens. I wasn't overly excited about going and may have even threatened, "If the car slows down, I'll jump out." My parents took my threats seriously.

Two guys from my youth group decided to attend the weekend as well. I don't think they were sent by their parents. They had actually chosen to go. I can't say for sure, but I think my parents may have asked these two guys to look after me, because they acted like bodyguards. On the drive to the retreat I had to sit in the back seat, sandwiched between them. My bodyguards stood about 6′7″ and 6′8″ each. Me on the other hand . . . let's just say I don't know what being 6′ feels like. They did their part, and I never jumped.

I ended up at this crazy, Jesus-loving Christian weekend with kids dressing weird and singing songs. The first day I hated it. It was a little out of my comfort zone, in more ways than one. The retreat took place at a remote location out in the woods. The thought of running away crossed my mind more than once. But then I remembered I wasn't that fast. Plus, getting back to the main road was quite the hike, and even if I got there, not many cars went by on a daily basis. So, I was stuck.

When we weren't singing silly songs or eating in the dining hall, we'd hear other students share about their lives. The first talk I heard was by a guy older than me who seemed to have it all together. He lived in the right town, came from the right family, played sports . . . but as he shared, he let us into his brokenness. Everything wasn't great. On the outside he held it together, but on the inside he was hurting. He let us into decisions he regretted, choices he wasn't proud of. He shared how he was trying to find the love of God.

I sat there listening, feeling for the first time not so alone. *I'm not the only one. He feels broken too.* Falsely, I had assumed that because this guy played sports he was living his dream. It never occurred to me that he could be struggling on the inside like I was. Different issues, same pain. As the weekend went on, others opened up and shared about their own brokenness. Others who looked healthy, who didn't have a degenerating disease.

Those I had put on a pedestal all of a sudden looked different, more vulnerable, as their walls came down and they got real about the struggles and brokenness they faced. By the end of the weekend we shared a common bond: we were all broken in one way or the other. The silly songs started to touch me in new ways, hugs weren't so creepy, and those I thought were weird became friends.

The other thing I realized at that Jesus-loving Christian weekend is that we are all in need of a Savior. That's what everyone talked about all weekend. Their need for a Savior. They had tried to fix things on their own, but that's not how it works. I started to understand I couldn't fix my brokenness on my own. As hard as I might possibly try, there's not a thing in the world I can do on my own to overcome muscular dystrophy. My body is broken. I had tried to deny it by holding on to my dreams of being a great athlete, and when that dream blew up in my face, the brokenness overwhelmed me.

Many of the kids at the retreat had circumstances that caused them incredible pain. I had MD while another guy I talked to had a raging, violent dad. Some kids came from abusive homes; some lived in a dangerous part of town where they witnessed things kids should never have to see. That weekend I saw that my brokenness extended beyond the disease that was starting to take over my body. It was more than the physical, emotional, and mental brokenness so many of us feel. What brought us all together was deeper than any of those things. We were all spiritually broken. I discovered that not only was my body sick and broken, but my soul was sick and broken as well. I'm talking about a deep, spiritual brokenness. My soul was aching. I needed a Savior.

Being broken hurts. I get it, trust me. But I also get the grace of God. The love of God. The forgiveness of God. The closeness of God. That's what I started to learn that weekend.

Scripture tells us, "The LORD is close to the brokenhearted; he rescues those whose spirits are crushed" (Psalm 34:18).

I finally saw I wasn't alone in this brokenness, and neither are you. We are all broken. I can confidently say that brokenness doesn't discriminate. No matter what we appear like on the outside, we are all broken and in a need of a Savior.

Friend, do you need rescuing? Are you brokenhearted? Are you exhausted from working so hard trying to figure it all out on your own? I want to encourage you with these healing words: "He heals the brokenhearted and binds up their wounds" (Psalm 147:3 NIV). We don't need to stay in the place of brokenness forever. The first step I had to take was to accept I was broken in many ways. That I didn't have it all together. If I couldn't recognize my brokenness—or a better way to say it—if I couldn't *admit* my brokenness, I would miss out on experiencing God's rescue.

God doesn't pull any punches when He tells us in His Word, "God opposes the proud but gives grace to the humble" (1 Peter 5:5). I was in danger of letting my ego get in the way of a life-giving, lifesaving, grace-filled relationship with Him. My eyes were finally opened that weekend. I finally recognized I was spiritually broken and I couldn't do squat on my own to fix it. I threw in the towel and fell into the arms of Jesus. He had been waiting.

PRAYER

Jesus, I'm tired. I'm exhausted. I see all of these images of people on social media and think they have it all together. I wonder what's wrong with me and why I don't have it all together. But I realize I am broken.

Jesus, your Word says you are close to the brokenhearted and you rescue those who are crushed in spirit. Jesus, I'm crushed in my spirit. Please fill me again with your Spirit. Help me understand. Let me feel the presence of your loving arms being wrapped around me. Jesus, mend me back together so that I may experience your grace and love, and that I may share your love with others.

In your precious name, Jesus,
Amen.

TRUE FOR ME

God heals my wounds when I am brokenhearted (PSALM 147:3).

God is with me and will give me courage (ISAIAH 41:10).

God is my refuge and strength (PSALM 46:1–2).

God will sustain me (PSALM 55:22).

God has overcome the world (JOHN 16:33).

God will not abandon me (2 CORINTHIANS 4:8–10).

God cares for me (1 PETER 5:7).

God will wipe away all my tears (REVELATION 21:4).

2

Battles with the Father

Did all the feelings of disappointment and hurt go away after that crazy, Jesus-loving Christian weekend? No. That's when the wrestling match began.

My prayers turned into downright, face-pinned-on-the-mat battles. *God, you're a God of love, they say. I've grown up hearing that. And yes, I have experienced your love at times. Yet I still have this incurable disease.* Although I had finally come to the point of recognizing I needed a Savior, I had a serious issue with God.

I couldn't understand how a loving God would leave me the way I was—broken. The Savior part made sense to me, but I couldn't see God as a father figure. I had heard others talk about God as a Father, a dad who loved them. "I can just climb up into His lap and talk with Him," they'd say. Those people felt loved and cared for; I could hear it in the way they described it. But I couldn't get there.

The idea of climbing into God's lap felt awkward at best. Climbing into my own dad's lap was never an option in my mind. He was an old, staunch Dutchman, and a redhead too, so that gives you an idea what kind of a temper he had. Back then, my dad didn't show feelings. He does now, thankfully, but not when I was a boy.

For some, picturing awkward dad hugs may bring up painful childhood memories, and I feel your pain. I've been in ministry long enough to know there are some not-so-nice dads out there who have caused a lot of damage, abusive fathers who will need to answer for their sin. Several people have confided in me over the years how much they struggle with seeing God as a loving Father because of how badly they've been treated by their own dad. I get it.

My dad wasn't abusive, just reserved. He didn't treat me badly. Yet I didn't think "Father" God was treating me very well either. I didn't think God liked me or cared much about my best interests. And I don't know about you, but when someone doesn't like me, I sure don't want to put my trust in them. All I could see was my broken self, and all I could hear was the persistent echo ringing through my head: *Why?* God seemed as though He was a million miles away, ignoring my question.

To add to my pain, my younger brother was coming up the ranks. Bill doesn't have the diagnosis. He's an able-bodied, good athlete. I had to watch my little brother become the athlete I had always dreamed of being. He was a three-sport athlete—football, basketball, baseball—and he was good at them all. When he quit football so he could run cross country, I thought he was the biggest dork I'd ever seen. You don't quit football to run cross country. But time and perspective change things. All these years later I think cross country is a pretty cool sport. In fact, my son ran cross country all through high school, qualifying for state, but back then I didn't even think it was a sport.

Besides Bill being the athlete I wanted to be, he and Dad were getting closer. Dad attended all Bill's events, and the two of them spent time together throwing the football or shooting hoops. I felt left out, neglected, and forgotten. I got so tired of feeling unnoticed and unloved while watching my brother have success. Rather than being happy for him, I was jealous. Instead of encouraging him, I was angry.

Jealousy wreaked havoc in my life. It filled me with bitterness and put up a barrier between my brother and me. I couldn't be proud of him because I wanted what he had. Since it pained me to go to his events, I isolated myself, escaping to unhealthy, dangerous habits to bring myself comfort. If you've ever felt this level of jealousy, you know what I'm talking about. The Bible talks about this kind of jealousy as well. "Anger is cruel, and wrath is like a flood, but jealousy is even more dangerous" (Proverbs 27:4). I was so jealous I didn't stay around for my brother's senior year to cheer him on. I look back now and wish I would've done it differently. In my hurt, I withdrew from everyone. Especially my dad.

Dad and I used to be close. That was back when we lived on the farm in Iowa. Until I was nine years old, our family lived on a farm near the small, rural town of Pella, Iowa. I didn't mind growing up in the middle of nowhere. In fact, I loved it.

To me, Iowa was the perfect place to live. But as I became an adult, I realized most people don't see it that way. Iowa gets no respect. As I travel around the country for speaking engagements, I get asked all the time, "Where do you live again? Idaho?"

"No, not Idaho. Iowa. I-o-wa. Not potatoes. Corn and soybeans. Iowa."

"Oh, I've heard of that. I think I flew over it once."

During those early years on the farm, I wasn't showing any symptoms of muscular dystrophy. My body still did what I wanted it to, and mostly that led to getting into trouble—like practicing bull riding on the hog or pretending to set our barn on fire and getting the entire Pella fire department to rush to our farm by mistake. I learned that when I wasn't with my dad, I got into trouble quite a bit. Not on purpose, mind you, but still.

Despite the mischief I got into, my dad and I had a special relationship on the farm. I went to the field with him nearly every day. Dad loved farming, and so did I. Mostly, I think, because I got to spend so much time with my dad. Farming was everything to me. It's what I loved the most. So when Dad sat us down to tell us we were leaving the farm, I didn't believe him.

He explained how he felt God was calling him into the ministry. I thought to myself, *You don't know anything about ministry, Dad. Plus, I've heard the vocabulary you use when you talk to the hogs. I don't think pastors are supposed to talk that way.* I tried to explain this to my dad, but my opinion didn't matter. Nothing would change his mind. I found myself battling with my own father over the thing I loved the most.

I didn't get to have a say in the decision to leave the farm. Someone else's decisions changed the direction of my life. It was such an awful, out-of-control feeling. Maybe you've been there. Maybe it was your family moving. Maybe it was your mom and dad deciding to go different directions. Maybe it was that night things got out of control and you were forced beyond what you were comfortable with.

What I learned that day is the terrible pain of being at the mercy of someone else's decisions. Since then, I've come to realize this is an unavoidable part of life, a natural result of being in relationship with other human beings. There will be times when another person's choice affects us. And there are times our choices affect other people as well. A friend once told me, "Nothing you do affects only you." That's good to remember.

Sometimes another person's decision can affect us in a good way. If the neighbor next door decides to put in a pool and you receive an open invitation to use it anytime you want, well, so be it. That's not so bad. But when someone makes a decision that causes you personal damage, a decision that forces you to give up something you love, a decision that affects you in a life-altering, heart-wrenching way . . . well, that's harder to take. My nine-year-old mind couldn't comprehend what was happening as moving trucks loaded up everything we owned and moved us from Iowa to Michigan so Dad could go to seminary. I only knew I had lost the thing I loved most in life—the farm—and I had no control over it.

I've been asked, "Who is to blame for leaving the farm, for taking away something you loved so dearly? Your dad or God? Or is it a little bit of both?"

For me it was both. I blamed God because He called my dad; plus, I was told He was in control of everything, so in my mind God could change things. And then I blamed my dad for going. It was a whole blame-game. An unstoppable ache squeezed my heart. I didn't know much about God at the time—I was only nine—but I didn't like the way I felt. I'm not sure I even understood the word *loss*, but something felt like it was gone.

Know What You're Battling

Having no other choice, I went from being a farm kid to a city kid. That's where my love for sports began.

During the Michael Jordan era, we all believed we could do anything.

"You can be anything you want to be!"
"If you put your mind to it, you can do it!"

Remember that? What a stupid, deceptive message. That's not even remotely true. Not everyone will be an athlete. Not everyone will be a doctor, a writer, a singer, whatever. Let's call a spade a spade and stop putting false dreams in kids' heads. Instead, let's help them understand the reality of the way things work. Not all dreams are achievable. It's important for kids to understand that. I know that can sound harsh, and I don't want to be a dream-destroyer. I do believe you can work hard and pull off impossible things. We see that played out every time an Olympic champion stands on the podium. Olympians show natural talent, typically at a young age, so they pursue a realistic goal based on their natural abilities. Makes sense. For the rest of us, however, instead of convincing ourselves we can accomplish anything, no matter how grand, we'll have a much more fulfilling future if we set realistic expectations. Let's help the kids in our lives understand reality from a young age. Setting realistic goals will lead to greater joy and contentment in their lives than if they grow up with unrealistic hopes.

Believe me. I know. If we're not careful, each of us has the potential to foster false hopes, things that just aren't meant to be. I'm not trying to be a pessimist; I'm just being real. I've learned it's futile to wrestle against the wrong thing. What I mean is this: you need to know what you're battling.

Sometimes we battle against natural laws. This happens when we try to force our lives to fit a design that simply makes no sense. If you can't sing, you're probably not going to win a Grammy. A 5′3″ gymnast isn't a likely candidate for heavyweight champion of the world. As a teen, I bought into all the positive "You can do it!" hype. I believed it so much that I bought Air Jordan basketball shoes so I could run faster and jump higher. I put up posters in my room of Michael soaring through the air and posters of Bo Jackson, the two-sport pro athlete (baseball and football). I even tried lifting weights. I told myself, *I'll work harder than ever, believe more, and not quit!*

And guess what?

It didn't work.

What I didn't understand at the time is that my muscles continued to deteriorate. Muscles are kind of important for an athlete. The laws of nature will win every time.

And let's recognize the futility of fighting against the basics of sowing and reaping, too, shall we? As much as we'd like to think otherwise, we will experience consequences from our own choices. When my dad went to seminary and I could no longer tag along with him, I pulled away. Then when he started spending more time with my athletic brother than he did with me, my attitude got sassy. In my mind he deserved it. I now recognize that Dad was being obedient to God's calling on his life, but as a kid I was mad at them both—Dad and God. I wanted to pin them both to the mat. As a result, I felt lonely and distant from my own dad, and I was barely on speaking terms with God. My loneliness was the result of my own actions. Reaping what I'd been sowing.

Another battle we need to be aware of is this one: like it or not, sin and evil exist in the world. The Enemy is hell-bent on preventing you from becoming the person the Father has created you to be. Each one of us encounters obstacles that are designed to trip us up, to divert our path away from God's best. Beware of those temptations that seem harmless. Trust me. There's an evil agenda to prevent you from fulfilling God's purpose for your life. Paul warned the Ephesians about that very thing. "For we are not fighting against flesh-and-blood enemies, but against evil rulers and authorities of the unseen world, against mighty powers in this dark world, and against evil spirits in the heavenly places" (Ephesians 6:12). Even jealousy can fit into this category. As I said, we need to know what we're battling.

My jealousy of my brother came from a selfish place within me. Not only did it directly go against what God wanted for me, it hurt my family as well. "For jealousy and selfishness are not God's kind of wisdom. Such things are earthly, unspiritual, and demonic. For wherever there is jealousy and selfish ambition, there you will find disorder and evil of every kind" (James 3:15–16). During high school, I didn't pay much attention to God's kind of wisdom.

The Bible is filled with spiritual examples of cause and effect as well. Joseph brags to his brothers, and they ship him and his colored coat off to Egypt as a slave (see Genesis 37). Pharoah makes a promise, then reneges on his word and loses everything in the process (see Exodus 12–14). Some consequences are positive. The apostles leave everything behind to follow Jesus and end up starting an eternal revolution. The more we read and study God's Word, the more we see how He has a divine plan for how things are supposed to work in this world. And that includes each one of us.

God has uniquely designed and gifted you, and if that's not to be a microbiologist or a social media influencer, it's okay. Instead of battling against God's design for you, I encourage you to lean into what He has created you to be. I fought that for the longest time. I ignored God's divine hand in my life, insisting I could still shape my life the way I wanted it to be.

By the time I was a freshman in high school, the symptoms of MD were showing up more and more. I collapsed in football practice, basketball practice, and got hit in the leg in baseball because I couldn't get out of the way of a pitch fast enough. My grit alone couldn't make my body do what I needed it to as an athlete. My second love—sports—was completely taken from me. First the farm, now sports. *Why, God? I mean, really, why?*

I began to believe that whatever I loved, God would take. *Oh, okay. I see how this works, God.* I loved the farm. My dad and I had a bond that was special. The farm and my closeness with my dad were in my past. Now I could add sports to my list of loves lost.

At the time, I didn't understand that God's ways are not always our ways. Through the prophet Isaiah, God says, "'For just as the heavens are higher than the earth, so my ways are higher than your ways and my thoughts higher than your thoughts'" (Isaiah 55:9). I also couldn't grasp that God actually wanted what was best for me, like in Romans 8:28: "And we know that God causes everything to work together for the good of those who love God and are called according to his purpose for them." This was a very confusing lesson for me to learn. I wrestled with questions I couldn't answer. What do you mean God's ways are higher than ours and for my good? Isn't "good for me" to be healed and make the team? Wouldn't good be to not have left the farm or to not be born with muscular dystrophy? And since I was already wrestling with whether God liked me or not, understanding that He was going to work everything together for my good seemed very unlikely.

I had more questions than I did answers. My battles with God raised a new series of questions: *God, am I bad person? Do bad things happen to bad people as well as good people?* That question really confused me because now I had no idea if I was bad or good.

My perspective on how God viewed me was based on my relationship with my father. I distanced myself from God just like I had from Dad. I believe this stemmed from a tragic sense of betrayal. Because my brother excelled in sports, I felt as though Dad loved my brother more than he loved me. I didn't hear words of praise from my dad, no "Good for you!" or "Good job!" I wasn't the athlete, so I didn't feel that I was receiving his love and attention, while Bill and Dad had a connection I envied. A whopper of a lie settled into my heart that made me want to knock God's eyes out. *That's why my brother doesn't have the disease. Because God loves him more—just like my dad loves my brother more than he loves me.*

So, I began to believe I was getting what I deserved. I sinned; therefore I was being punished. The punishment was to take away from me what I loved. I must be a bad person. God didn't love me or want anything to do with me. What hurt even more was I falsely believed God loved everyone more than me. Especially my brother. *God, why did my brother not get this disease? The jealousy is killing me. Why does his road look so much easier to walk? Do you love him more? Does adversity in my life mean I'm living wrong and you're using it to get my attention?*

Whether God was using adversity to get my attention or not can be argued, but what can't be argued is that everyone experiences storms. Even my star athlete brother. He had to deal with the pain of rejection from his jealous older brother, for starters.

Storms don't play favorites. They don't care whether you come from Iowa or Idaho. It matters not how much talent you have or don't have. Jesus tells us that the rain, winds, and floods come, and whether we are able to withstand the storms or not depends on where we have built our foundation (or life)—on the rock or on the sand. The rock is able to hold up against the torrents and the rising flood waters, but if you build your life on the sand, when the winds and floods come, it collapses with a mighty crash (see Matthew 7:24–27). I was headed for a crash.

I kept pushing myself, but I didn't know what I was up against, not really. Even though I knew I had muscular dystrophy, I couldn't grasp it entirely as a young teen.

While my brother was fulfilling his dream (and my dream too), I went to climb the stairs one day at our high school and couldn't. Just yesterday I could, but not today. What was going on? *God, you have the farm, you have sports. And now I can't even climb steps?! What more do you want?* My anger and pain grew deeper and deeper.

My heart was so broken. I couldn't find answers to all the questions I had inside. *Why? Why is this my life?* I've learned that questions can kill you too.

Wrestling Isn't Wrong

I had always been taught that there was a heaven and a hell, and every time I looked in the mirror, I saw hell. I hated life. I hated me. I hated almost everything around me. I just really didn't like myself. I reached the point where I believed the only option for me was to take my life.

So one night I put a rope around my neck. Thoughts of suicidal despair overwhelmed me. *I'm done. I hurt. I don't want to hurt anymore. I don't really get along with my family anyway. Everything I have loved seems to have been taken from me, so, yeah, God . . . I'm done.*

I don't remember what had happened that day to make me feel like ending it all. Everything was changing, and I couldn't handle any more losses. Plus, I was tired of not measuring up, of not being able to accomplish my dreams. At that moment, I cried out, "God, I want to die. I don't get any of this."

I sat in the bathroom and stared at the rope in my hands. I don't know where I found the rope or what it was for. I just knew it was strong enough to do what I needed it to do. It's surprising how even a little rope can close off your ability to breathe.

But as I got close to unconsciousness, I started thinking . . . *What comes next?*

I didn't know.

I believed there was a heaven and hell, and since I was already living in hell, I sure didn't want to spend eternity there. I was too scared to die.

So I released the rope, and I sat in the dark bathroom, screaming on the inside. *Aaaaargh! I wish I was strong enough to complete this! But I'm not.*

The fear that I didn't know where I would end up was the only thing that made me let go of the rope that night.

From that point, I became rebellious, angry, even violent in a way. I was a hurting kid.

I wanted to live; I just didn't want to live broken.

I also wanted to know that I was loved, that I belonged . . . but I didn't act like it. I developed an awful attitude, rebelling against almost everything. My philosophy became: you can kick me out, suspend me, tell me I can't be a part of it, and I won't care. I felt as though I had nothing else to lose. Everything I wanted was already gone.

I couldn't find or understand a God of love. My dad talked about one every Sunday when he preached, but it wasn't making sense to me. I understood a God of punishment, distance, and anger. I was afraid of Him, truth be told. God and I were stuck in an ultimate wrestling match. I was sick of being hurt and disappointed by Him. I'd shake my fist at Him in anger. *God, the Bible talks about you being a God of miracles, yet I can no longer climb stairs. And the doctors tell me I'll be in a wheelchair full-time by the time I'm thirty. God, where's my miracle? I mean, Moses got a burning bush and a sea to part for him. Can't I get a little something?* I was spitting mad, and I couldn't see any way around it. My battles with God the Father didn't end overnight.

There are many things that simply don't make sense on this earth. My faith has been tattered and tested time and time again. But I hold on to Psalm 23:4: "Even when I walk through the darkest valley, I will not be afraid, for you are close beside me. Your rod and your staff protect and comfort me." I've walked through those valleys and deserts. In the darkest places I have cried out to God, while at the same time wanting nothing to do with Him.

To be honest, for a long time I thought He wanted nothing to do with me. And then He'd reach out in His gentle, subtle way to show me He hadn't forgotten me. It seemed that at just the right times, God would give me a glimmer of hope that He loved me. I'd catch the lyrics to a song on the radio, words that pierced my heart. Or a person from church would speak into my life with something like "Rob you're here for a reason." I wasn't sure what that reason was, but it gave me a sense of purpose to keep going.

As I've matured, I've come to know the love of God in a real and personal way. Even like a child to a father. Because that's how He loves us. "See what great love the Father has for us that He would call us His children. And that is what we are" (1 John 3:1 NLV). A Father whose lap is safe to crawl into.

If you're in a wrestling match with God, don't give up. We can learn a thing or two from Jacob about wrestling with God. The famous wrestling match takes place in the Old Testament just as Jacob is returning home, hopefully to make amends with his older twin brother, Esau. Jacob is kind of afraid of Esau, and for good reason if you ask me. Many years earlier, Jacob duped his big bro out of his birthright over a bowl of soup. Now, on his way back home, Jacob wants to make sure God hasn't forgotten His promise to bless Jacob with great success and countless descendants. He is Abraham's grandson, after all. God's promise couldn't be fulfilled if Esau kills him. So Jacob prays and reminds God of His promise and demands a blessing, wrestling with God all night until he receives it. Jacob wouldn't give up until God blessed him (see Genesis 32:22–32).

God rewards His persistent wrestling partner with a blessing and a new name, Israel. Plus, Esau welcomes his little brother with open arms (see Genesis 33). God keeps His promise to Jacob. He is chosen, not forgotten, and blessed.

There is purpose in your wrestling. It takes faith to wrestle. God's shoulders are big enough to handle your questions, your anger, and your doubt. Wrestling isn't wrong. It means there's something deep in your soul longing for what only God can provide.

PRAYER

Father God, I'm grateful that you don't give up on me! You see the whole picture while I only get a glimpse of it all. At times, that glimpse isn't enough for me, and doubts and questions flood my mind. My heart aches when I experience loss, when I don't understand your plan. Jesus, give me faith as I walk through the hills and valleys of life. Give me the strength to hold on to hope and believe you love me and walk with me in the darkest moments of my life. Thank you for loving me.
In Jesus' name,
Amen.

TRUE FOR ME

God loves me (JOHN 3:16).

God allows me to wrestle with Him (HOSEA 12:3–5).

God's love is better than life (PSALM 63:3).

God's presence brings me joy (PSALM 16:11).

The Holy Spirit is with me in my trials, building my perseverance (JAMES 1:2–4).

God's glory in me will be greater than my suffering (ROMANS 8:17–18).

God will never abandon me or let me be defeated (2 CORINTHIANS 4:7–9).

God renews my spirit in the middle of trouble (2 CORINTHIANS 4:16–18).

God will rescue me (2 CORINTHIANS 1:8–10).

God's victory in me will last forever (2 CORINTHIANS 4:17).

God gives me strength when I am weary (ISAIAH 40:27–29).

God will answer my cry (JEREMIAH 33:3).

Jesus sets an example for me to persevere (HEBREWS 12:1–3).

3

The Lies We Believe

As a young man, I not only wrestled with God . . . I wrestled with who I was. Our society demands perfection, I believed, and I was far from it. Without the ability to excel in what mattered the most to me—farming, sports, girls (okay, I might be lying about that last one)—I believed I would never fit in, never succeed. At anything. I'd be the guy others pitied, and I hated that. The lies kept me angry, stuck, without hope. In today's culture there seem to be even more ugly lies than ever, outrageous lies that threaten our identity, our faith, our soul. And they will easily seep into our minds if we're not careful.

The lying whispers (or sometimes shouts) we allow ourselves to believe never amount to anything good. And here's the dangerous part . . . we don't always recognize the lies. A guy tells me it must be hard for me to be in a wheelchair. Words of compassion, he thinks. Accusations of me being a burden is what I hear. Just enough truth in his innocent comment for a lie to latch on to. Or maybe, like me, you've had thoughts of insecurity, of not measuring up, and you didn't have enough evidence to argue yourself out of that mess. I can't change a car tire; that's true, but that doesn't mean I'm less of a man than the burly guy who stops to change my flat on the side of the road. It's just enough truth with garbage tacked on that I am tempted to believe it. That's the way sneaky lies work. We don't always see them coming, and they ooze their way into our hearts and minds before we know it. And the longer we listen to the lies, the more we believe them.

Here's something important to remember about lies: We know where they come from. The Bible talks about the Evil One, the devil prowling around like a roaring lion looking for someone to devour (see 1 Peter 5:8).

Well, his roars were devouring me.

Being handicapped was killing me on the inside and killing my faith in God. Every day was a battle between good and evil. In Jesus we find truth and life and light and goodness. In Satan we find destruction. And lies. "The devil has nothing to do with the truth. There is no truth in him. It is expected of the devil to lie, for he is a liar and the father of lies" (John 8:44 NLV). So why in the world would we believe lies, knowing the source? Because, like I said, they're sneaky. Lies often seem to make sense. Sometimes they are partially true. Like our buddy Jacob in the previous chapter. His wrestling match with God awarded him with a disjointed hip and a limp for the rest of his life. The truth of that part of Jacob's story can cause us to believe God isn't safe, that He punishes those who don't toe the line. Only God knows why He inflicted Jacob with a handicap. I can only speculate that maybe God understood the ambitious young leader's tendency to forge ahead on his own, that Jacob needed a reminder of his dependency on God for the heavy responsibility that lay ahead of him. God chose Jacob as the head of an entire line of God's chosen people, Israel.

It is not in God's character to beat people down or hold us back. He consistently tells us throughout Scripture that He wants the best for us. The best! "'For I know the plans I have for you,' says the LORD. 'They are plans for good and not for disaster, to give you a future and a hope'" (Jeremiah 29:11). Yet we so often forget this truth, looking instead at the evidence of limps and hitches and failures all around us with our limited human understanding. The lies that keep us feeling forgotten, unseen, unloved make so much sense. And at times, the lies fuel our already beaten-down self-image. That's what happened to me.

I listened to the lies for a long time, way longer than I should have, and long enough for them to shape my beliefs as a teen. I believed the lies that I was different, I was a nobody, I'd never be loved, and for absolute certain, I'd never amount to anything. My friend, if you can relate, I'm sorry, and I understand. But there is hope, I assure you.

Lie 1: I'm Different and That's Bad

One of the sneakiest lies almost all of us get sucked into is the nagging "I'm different from others, and being different is a bad thing." Somehow we buy into the lie that the norm holds all the cards to happiness. And because we see ourselves as different from all the "normal" people in the world, we assume we've been dealt a bad deck. The lie convinces us that different equals bad, less than, unable to compete. We may as well raise the white flag and give up, wallow in the lie that we're different and that's irreparably bad.

To be upset about that actually doesn't make much sense. Well, of course we are different! Just like snowflakes or clouds or bumps on a toad, each of us is unique. Yet, as human beings we tend to set ourselves up against some ideal standard—some perfect image of what others are able to achieve that the rest of us sorry saps can't live up to. Do you know what I mean? Handsome and beautiful get the spotlight; intelligent and aggressive get the executive position; wealthy and ambitious get the best toys; the most athletic get the fame; and the rest of us who don't find ourselves in one of those categories end up thinking that because we're different, we're not as good, not as valuable, not as lovable.

Getting lapped while running the mile in sixth grade was one of the most humiliating moments in my life. Not only had my body let me down, but I also realized for the first time I was different.

And in our society, different isn't good.

This wasn't about running (or failing to run) a mile in gym class; it was about my identity and where I fit in with everyone else. As much as I wanted to remain carefree and hang around with my buddies as if nothing had happened, the diagnosis of muscular dystrophy could no longer go unnoticed. I now had to carry the stigma of being different. For me, being different came with the lie that I was inferior. In my mind, I simply didn't have the same value as the guy who could make his muscles work.

The next six years were a roller coaster of emotions and setbacks for me. Although the disease was progressing, I did everything I could to hide it. When my dad moved us to his second church in a different town halfway through my junior year, I told him he couldn't tell anyone his son had muscular dystrophy. For the most part, from the outside I looked pretty normal, but getting up off the floor, running, or climbing stairs would give me away. So I got good at hiding it. I'd get to the football or basketball game extra early before anyone else arrived so no one could see me struggle as I climbed the empty bleachers. I didn't climb them like a normal person would. I could go down the bleachers or steps, just not up them. Figure that one out.

It didn't take me long to realize other people couldn't handle my being different. When I told one high school friend about the diagnosis, I saw something die in his eyes.

Before he could say a word, I blurted, "You don't wanna be friends anymore, do you?"

He replied with a straight face, "Nope, I don't want to have to worry about you."

And that was it. I started to equate being different with rejection—being thrown out, useless—or worse, a burden. It would take many years, heartaches, and tears to realize that belief was a big fat lie.

At the time, I couldn't yet see the bigger picture of God's design, how He created each of us with a purpose, quirks and all. Even the weak ones who can only climb down bleachers. God has a master plan that includes the weak, the strong, the witty, the slow, and everyone in between. We all make up the body of Christ, each of us in our own unique way. I eventually learned a biblical truth about this that helped me. I think you'll like it too. God has a soft spot in His heart for those the world tends to look down on for being different or less than. He sees our value. When Paul described the body of Christ and the importance of its parts, he shows God's heart for people like you and me. Paul says, "In fact, some parts of the body that seem weakest and least important are actually the most necessary" (1 Corinthians 12:22).

But, like I said, I couldn't see that at the time. It took me a long time to accept that I just might qualify as "actually the most necessary." I couldn't fathom God's purpose for me as a teen. The pain of being different from everyone else sank so deep, I started cutting my arms with a ruler in an attempt to distract myself from the pain. I wanted to get attention, for someone to tell me I was okay the way I was. Not different, please.

There was something else too. It wasn't just my body that failed me. I felt like God Himself had let me down. He was the one responsible for this whole mess to begin with. He made me who I was and put me where I could be humiliated. He had made me weak. I couldn't comprehend why God would do this to me. Instead of running into His arms, I tried to run as far away from them as fast as I could (in my mind I can run much faster than I can in reality. . . . And I look like Matthew McConaughey with sixpack abs too. Just sayin'). All through high school I was trying to figure out who I was, what God wanted from me, and why I was put on this earth.

I just couldn't believe I had a loving Father who held great plans for me. The lie I believed felt hopeless: I was different, which meant I wasn't as valuable as others. What I failed to recognize at that time in my life, and what I want to remind you of today, is that each of us is a unique creation made by God's own hands. Yes, we're different. And that's the beauty of who we are. Just like a carefully crafted piece of pottery on the Master's wheel— individually and carefully created with loving attention. "Yet you, LORD, are our Father. We are the clay, you are the potter; we are all the work of your hand" (Isaiah 64:8 NIV). We are different, and that's good. Very good.

Lie 2: I'm a Nobody

Even worse than feeling different is feeling like a nobody. The person who walks into a room and no one seems to notice. The one whose name "accidentally" gets left off the invitation list. The guy who still has desires and needs but is convinced he'll never get the chance to fulfill them because he's a nobody. Feeling like a nobody is a lie that rubs us raw. Leaves us hopeless. Who cares about a nobody?

In the rural community where I grew up, if you're not an athlete, you're a nobody. It's that simple. Shoot, I wasn't even a band geek.

I felt so unseen. My identity had taken a fatal hit. I was far from the sports hero catching the eye of the cheerleaders. I was more like the guy who had to stay after the game and clean up trash under the bleachers. Even that didn't happen. I felt invisible. Unseen. Unloved. Did anyone even know I existed? How could they? I was a nobody.

In my brokenness I tried to establish a new identity for myself. I started going to parties. I drank a lot of beer during those days, even though I'd been taught alcohol was taboo. Truth is, I didn't like being sober. When I was sober I felt pain and confusion inside. I'd show up at parties with a cigarette behind each ear, a dip in my lip, and a cigarette hanging out of my mouth. I just wanted to fit in somewhere.

During the height of my rebellion, God showed me He hadn't forgotten about me and that I was somebody worth caring about. I attended DC 91, the Congress on Youth Evangelism with a bunch of dorks (what I called them) from my church. I mostly went because of the girls. But as I listened to the Christian comedian Ken Davis share the gospel, the truth of God's love for me began to break the stronghold of lies. I went down to the front for prayer, and out of more than fifteen thousand people in the convention center, the first person to meet me was my volunteer youth leader.

She smiled at me. "Rob, we've been praying for this day for a long time."

I looked at her with my smug, smirky little face.

"Well, I didn't ask you to."

The sting of that statement swirled inside me. *I never asked to be here. I never asked to be put on this earth. I never asked to be made, for sure not like this. None of it.* At the same time, her words were something I desperately needed to hear. Someone saw me. Someone cared about me. Someone prayed for me. You don't do that for a nobody.

At the crazy, Jesus-loving weekend a few years earlier, I had learned that other people were broken, just like me. At this conference, I learned that I'm not a nobody in Jesus' eyes, and I asked Him into my heart to be my Savior. I wish I could tell you everything changed in an instant, that I became a model Christian. I didn't. But it was a start.

I'm not going to lie to you, especially in a chapter about lies—there are times I still fight the lies of feeling like a nobody, of being "less than." This happens especially when I have felt overlooked, which happens often, unfortunately. For example, on a recent family vacation with my wife and kids, we picked a city that is known for being accessibility friendly. Hungry and excited to be off the plane, we headed to a highly recommended restaurant. When we arrived, we saw the restaurant perched on stilts with stairs for their able-bodied guests. I would need to use the elevator to get up to the restaurant. And then we found out the elevator hadn't worked in two years. The feeling of being overlooked crept in. We went to another restaurant that allegedly had an entrance ramp. The excitement of vacation was back! Until we discovered the blocked ramp being used to store all the extra chairs. In times like these, I feel overlooked, and I have to fight the lie that I am a nobody who is not worth caring about. In these moments, I take a deep breath and pray, asking Jesus to remind me how much He cares about me. He always does. He reminds me I'm not a nobody, and neither are you.

Lie 3: I'll Never Be Loved

Being unlovable is one of the Enemy's most hurtful lies because each of us has a desperate need to be loved. That's one of the reasons Jesus tells us to love one another the same way He loves us (see John 13:34). He sees our need for love, for community, to belong. And how does He love us? With a love that has no end. "'I have loved you, my people, with an everlasting love. With unfailing love I have drawn you to myself'" (Jeremiah 31:3). Over the years, I have experienced the love of God through my Christian community over and over in the middle of my brokenness. The same can be true for you. I'm here to tell you wholeheartedly: to believe we'll never be loved is a lie.

In my dark teen years, I resisted letting anyone get too close to me. An overwhelming fear of rejection kept me trapped in a destructive lie. I believed my brokenness made me unlovable. My body didn't work right; therefore, I was not worthy of being loved. If you've ever felt this way, I pray you will be able to see that stinkin' lie for what it is. No matter how hard the Enemy tries to prevent God's love from reaching us, it can't be done. "No power in the sky above or in the earth below—indeed, nothing in all creation will ever be able to separate us from the love of God that is revealed in Christ Jesus our Lord" (Romans 8:39). You are loved!

It meant a lot to me that my youth group leaders cared about me, that I wasn't a nobody in their eyes. But let's be real. That's not quite the same as being seen, I mean, really being seen by a girl. I never believed there was a woman in her right mind who would love somebody like me. Until I met Sharla.

I first saw her while I was sitting in the high school library, a rarity for me. Libraries and I didn't get along all that well. I liked to talk more than I liked to study, and librarians usually like it quiet in there. I suppose I went to the library to scope out the girls; I doubt I went there to actually read. I was sitting as far away from the librarian as possible when a beautiful blonde with blue eyes and a bubbly personality walked in. *That's a girl I'd like to date!* We didn't. But we did become friends, until I graduated and left town.

I went to Arizona for college and to try to figure out who I was. Many a day and night I cried out to God: "What do you want from me?" "Why did you make me?" "What am I supposed to do with my life?" Most days I still felt like a nobody who was different from everybody else. Lies and questions filled my mind day after day, especially the ones that haunted me the most: *Will someone ever love me? Who in their right mind would love a guy with my disease?*

God has a way of working that still surprises me. After being in the Arizona desert for a few months, I went back home for a retreat. Sharla and I reconnected, which was a miracle in and of itself. Even though she was working at the retreat, I didn't see her until after it was all over. She needed a ride to the airport, just the destination where my parents were taking me. We offered her a ride, and after a few conversations in the car, at the airport, and a handful of phone calls between Iowa and Arizona, we quickly realized we were meant to be together. I returned to Arizona, quit school, then went back home to Iowa, knowing I was going to marry this girl. She was my dream girl from the first time I saw her walk into the library that day back in high school.

We got engaged within a few months, and shortly after that, we got married. Yes, we married young, but we wanted to start our life together as soon as possible. Lurking in the background was a disease that wasn't going away.

But you know what did go away? The lie that I would never be loved. Sharla's love for me crushed that lie. I never knew such bold, selfless love could exist, the kind of love that recites the wedding vows "in sickness and in health" knowing full well sickness has already entered the picture.

I have learned to rise above adversity because Sharla has taught me what love looks like with no strings attached. That's unconditional love and the way God loves us as well. He loves us in the middle of our mess. "But God is so rich in mercy, and he loved us so much, that even though we were dead because of our sins, he gave us life when he raised Christ from the dead" (Ephesians 2:4–5). We can't earn God's love. And no lie can prevent His love from reaching us.

I have often said that Sharla shows me the love of Jesus every day. The idea no one would ever love me was an outright lie, and it is a lie for you as well. The very essence of God is love, and those who walk through life in relationship with God will know His love. His love is for each one of us. "So we have come to know and to believe the love that God has for us. God is love, and whoever abides in love abides in God, and God abides in him" (1 John 4:16 ESV). I don't know how God will show His love for you, who He will bring into your life or when, but I do know we can trust God for a life filled with love. It's who He is.

Lie 4: I'll Never Amount to Anything

As children, we have such happy hopes and dreams, and we believe with all our little cowboy hearts those things will come true. Until we grow up and hit real life. For some of us, when we start to realize those dreams just ain't happenin', we assume it's because of us. We must have done something wrong or worse (gulp), we're not good enough. We don't handle our relationships right, our attitude stinks, we make bonehead decisions, we harbor nasty thoughts about someone we just don't like, and our character isn't as holy as we wish it was. We are haunted by mistakes we've made in the past and terrified by our shortcomings today. And the lie "I'll never amount to anything" seeps into our souls. This is a brokenness so many of us can relate to.

Some of us had tougher beginnings than others. A tough childhood, a tough school experience, a tough first job, a tough marriage, or a tough past can make our future seem bleak. We believe the lie that since we haven't arrived at much so far, how could we ever amount to anything going forward? Any one of us, whether we've been through tough times or not, can get hoodwinked by this lie. It takes hope to believe we can amount to anything, and hope isn't always easy to come by.

I had always wanted to be a farmer, but my body would never have the strength to fulfill that dream. That's not a lie. That's my reality. And my dream of being a professional athlete flopped before I started shaving. That's not a lie either. But other lies piggybacked onto these major disappointments in my life. I started to believe I would never amount to anything. Who would hire a guy, knowing before long he would be in a wheelchair? It felt as though everything was stacked against me. The career paths I wanted weren't options. I could talk myself out of possibilities before I ever started. *You're disabled. You can't reach that. You can't get out of the car yourself. Someone will always have to be with you, and I'm sure they don't want to hire two people. The*

47

company will have to make changes they don't want to make. All the negative self-talk ended up snowballing into an ugly lie: "I'll never amount to anything."

I know for a fact this lie comes at us from so many angles for different people: Not enough money. Not enough education. Not funny or charming. Not a strong leader. Not a good goal-setter or planner. These are examples of obstacles that trap us in lies of defeat. So much of our personal worth stems from our accomplishments. At least that's how we humans measure things. On God's scale, it doesn't matter what we accomplish; He loves us for who we are. Still, He calls us to put forth our best efforts and work diligently. I wanted to work hard; I was willing to work hard. I just didn't believe I could work hard enough to ever amount to anything.

God proved the lies wrong. Near the end of college, I confided in my brother that I felt God was calling me to start a ministry, that I was supposed to go tell my story.

With instant support, he suggested, "Why don't you call it RISE? You have a hard time rising."

"All right. Done."

So in 2001, I started working on this thing called RISE Ministries. It began with me telling my story around town, and the ministry grew from there. Over the years we have welcomed tens of thousands of guests at RiseFest, our annual live Christian music festival held in northwest Iowa. I've traveled and spoken to audiences around the country and internationally. RISE Ministries hosts a podcast, produces videos, partners with other ministries that reach across the globe, and that's just the beginning. Only God can say what else He wants this "different nobody who won't amount to anything" to do.

And God wants to say that same thing to you. Don't buy in to the lie that you'll never amount to anything. You are God's child, priceless in the Father's eyes. The apostle Paul says, "And since we are his children, we are his heirs. In fact, together with Christ we are heirs of God's glory" (Romans 8:17). As a child of God, you can amount to more than you could ever imagine.

I'm a simple farm boy from Iowa, yet God has done great things. Not because I did, or am, anything special, but because of His work in and through me (and lots of other amazing people who make RISE Ministries happen). When we let ourselves be defeated by the lie "I'll never amount to anything," we allow the lie to become truth. We can obliterate the lies by seeing the truth through God's eyes, by renewing our minds in Him.

How to Renew Your Mind

The devil screams lies at us all the time. But how do you and I fight them? First, we need to stop listening to them. Yes, I know. That's easier said than done. So, I'm going to show you how to stop those lies in their evil tracks with four undefeatable ways to renew your mind—prayer, praise, Scripture, and healthy community.

Renew Your Mind in Prayer

When lies have the upper hand, they cause us a lot of anxiety. Instead of letting anxiety separate us from the truth, we can let it prompt us to pray. Our first step of renewing our minds is to strongarm that anxiety by handing it over to Jesus. "Cast all your anxiety on him because he cares for you" (1 Peter 5:7 NIV). We do that in prayer.

Prayer is such a unique and personal gift from God. It's the opportunity for us to connect with God and lay out what's on our hearts. More than once I have relied on this beautiful truth: "Don't worry about anything; instead, pray about everything. Tell God what you need, and thank him for all he has done. Then you will experience God's peace, which exceeds anything we can understand. His peace will guard your hearts and minds as you live in Christ Jesus" (Philippians 4:6–7). Whenever I start to feel overwhelmed or the old lies start to take hold again, I stop and spend some time in prayer. And just like God promises, my mind is renewed as He guards my heart and mind by kicking the lies to the curb.

Prayer is a powerful lie-buster. The Bible tells us that prayer has the power to heal, to forgive others and to receive forgiveness from God ourselves, to bring answers, to move mountains, to calm the storms—and to drown out the lies. Jesus says, "I am the way and the truth and the life" (John 14:6 NIV). Jesus is the truth! Truth exposes lies and tosses them out like yesterday's trash. The more time we spend talking with Jesus, which is what prayer is, the more familiar we become with truth, which exposes the lies for what they are. When we take the time to listen in prayer, the lies are drowned out by the simple small voice of the one who loves us most—Almighty God.

Renew Your Mind with Praise

Praise is all about perspective. When I focus on what can go wrong or why my life isn't fair, depression, hopelessness, and despair set in. My glass becomes half-empty instead of half-full. In a way, I'm giving honor to all the negative possibilities. What a waste of time and energy! But when I choose to praise God in the midst of challenges, it changes my perspective.

Last year (okay, lots of years) at RiseFest, the weather report looked rough. Severe weather possibilities, rain, lightning, damaging wind—all the things you don't want to be in the forecast for an outdoor event. I did have a plan, of course. If the weather hit quick, I'd first make sure everyone else got to the safety shelter. Being out in the open, making sure everyone else made it to safety, I might not have a lot of time to react. Plus, I'm not steady on my feet. So I had a plan in case the wind should blow me over in the process. If the wind knocked me to the ground, I was going to have Sharla back the minivan over me and I'd ride out the storm underneath it. Sharla was quick to point out it wasn't a very good plan. She was right, of course, so instead of constantly worrying about what might happen, I praised God for what He was doing and for how He had been faithful in the past. As I prayed, I felt my spirit and my mind being renewed. The festival went on.

One of the reasons we praise God is because of His unconditional love for us. Knowing He loves us while we're in the valley as much as He does while we're on the top of the mountain motivates us to praise Him. Praising God shifts our focus from the lies to the truth. It renews our mind with the truth of who He is: He is good, He is mighty, He created all things, He is full of grace and mercy, He is sovereign, He is faithful, He is all powerful, all-knowing, all-seeing . . . the list is limitless because God is limitless.

Prayer and praise help us remember who we are and whose we are. Lies don't stand a chance against that. Prayer allows us to stop focusing on our circumstances and turn our attention to Him. One of my favorite ways to do that is to praise Jesus through worship with music. When I praise Him, my heart goes from empty to full. No, I'm not always walking around singing out loud, but if you happen to see me in the car, well . . . that's another story.

Whatever you are facing, I invite you to praise our praiseworthy God along with the psalmist right now:

> Shout with joy to the LORD, all the earth!
> Worship the LORD with gladness.
> Come before him, singing with joy.
> Acknowledge that the LORD is God!
> He made us, and we are his.
> We are his people, the sheep of his pasture.
> Enter his gates with thanksgiving;
> go into his courts with praise.
> Give thanks to him and praise his name.
> For the LORD is good.
> His unfailing love continues forever,
> and his faithfulness continues to each generation.
>
> Psalm 100:1–5

Renew Your Mind with Scripture

Scripture is more than a collection of books written over two thousand years ago. It has big-time relevancy for today. The Bible says, "For the word of God is alive and powerful. It is sharper than the sharpest two-edged sword, cutting between soul and spirit, between joint and marrow. It exposes our innermost thoughts and desires" (Hebrews 4:12). Scripture exposes the lies that creep into our minds. It also reminds us of who we are and whose we are. As the lies scream in my ear, "You are less than others because you're different"; "You are a nobody"; "Nobody will ever love you"; and "You'll never amount to anything," Romans 8:37 (NIV) repeats from my lips, "No, in all these things we are more than conquerors through him who loved us." "For we are God's masterpiece. He has created us anew in Christ Jesus, so we can do the good things he planned for us long ago" (Ephesians 2:10). That would be good for each of us to hear every day.

We all understand the concept of garbage in, garbage out. What we fill our head with is what we start believing and reflecting. There's a lot of garbage (aka lies) floating around in our world today on social media, news outlets, movies, and TV. We hear lies that support the Enemy's garbage everywhere we go. That's why it is so important for us to spend time reading our Bibles, renewing our minds with God's truth. In His Word we find strength, confidence, and courage to stand firm against the lies. There's a reason the Word of God is referred to as a sword. It's our best weapon.

Renew Your Mind in a Healthy Community

One of the best ways to renew our minds, to feel seen, loved, and not forgotten is in community. Community has always been important. Jesus traveled with His disciples, and when He sent them out, He paired them two by two. The Bible tells us that, "For where two or three are gathered together in My name, there I am with them" (Matthew 18:20 NLV). Sounds like a community to me.

But somewhere along the way, the idea that "I can do it on my own," has clouded our perspective. Our culture prizes independence. And hiding in isolation provides the perfect breeding ground for the Enemy's lies. It's easier to listen to the lying whispers when there's no one else around to remind us of the truth. We're not meant to walk this journey of faith alone. The Bible tells us, "And let us consider how we may spur one another on toward love and good deeds, not giving up meeting together, as some are in the habit of doing, but encouraging one another—and all the more as you see the Day approaching" (Hebrews 10:24–25 NIV). In community, we spur one another on to walk in God's truth. We've got this!

Although community is important, there is a difference between healthy and unhealthy community. Healthy community builds you up. It adds value to your life, challenges you where you need to be challenged, and is life-giving. It walks alongside you in the good and the bad, when life is beautiful and when it's broken. Those in healthy community pray for you and let you pray for them. You can confide in them.

Unhealthy community is usually about the other person. Those in unhealthy community have negative attitudes; they're not afraid to complain or explain how their life is unfair and everybody's out to get them. Instead of being life-giving, they can be life-sucking. No matter how hard you try, it's never quite good enough. And they can't be trusted with your deep, dark secrets. Bottom line: an unhealthy community walks in lies instead of God's truth.

Even though I had been somewhat of a rebel in high school, God allowed me to graduate with my head held high. I felt seen, loved, and intentionally not forgotten.

All because of community.

Our principal, Mr. Bob, called me in for a conversation one day about graduation. He had heard a rumor that I wasn't planning on attending. I explained to him that the rumor was true. I planned to avoid it because our graduation ceremony (like so many others) consisted of us graduates walking into the gym, sitting in chairs, and then when our name was called, climbing up the steps by the stage and walking across the stage to receive our diploma. There was only one problem—steps.

Mr. Bob discreetly approached the shop instructor with fresh instructions to build a couple of ramps for graduation, not steps. No reasons given. My name wasn't ever brought up. Because of Mr. Bob's sensitivity to my situation, I didn't miss my high school graduation. I was there with all my classmates. Took pictures with my friends. Talked about how long we'd waited for this day. Finally, I was done with high school. Praise the Lord! I walked proudly across the stage, stopped to get my diploma and take a picture for the school yearbook, took a quick peek to make sure my diploma was signed, shook Mr. Bob's hand, and went back to my seat. Then I was off to my party to have some cake and ice cream and celebrate with friends and family—my community.

Today, so many years later, there are at least five guys in my life (my community) because I physically need them. As much as I hate needing help, I also get to see the beauty of receiving it. We're there for each other. These guys help renew my mind by showing me the beauty of being a part of the body of Christ. They make me feel loved, seen, and remembered.

When I think of these things, my heart fills with praise to God because I know I'm not alone. Life is hard, but it's also beautiful, especially when we let people into it.

Friend, through the hope we find in Jesus we have the power to overcome every stinkin' lie. When you start to think of your differences as bad, remember how God sees you—beautifully unique, treasured, adored. If you sense the old lie of being unworthy, a nobody, remind yourself that Jesus loves you so much

He gave His life for you. In those lonely moments when the nagging fear of never being loved haunts you, call to mind the words of God as He whispers to you gently, "I have loved you with an everlasting love" (Jeremiah 31:3 NIV). Think of God's purpose for your life when you start to worry about the future. His dreams for us will be more fulfilling than any dream we could conjure up on our own. Hold on tight to God's Word with me, will you? Let's invite His truth to continually renew our mind, filling us with the discernment to recognize the lies and replace them with God's renewing love.

PRAYER

Jesus, help me to remember I don't need to do it on my own. I'm not made to do it alone. I need others. Please bring people into my life who can help, and help me be that person for someone else. Jesus, don't let me believe the lies of the Evil One. Give me the strength to hold on to the truth that I am loved, I am seen, and I am known by the Father.

In your precious name, Jesus,
Amen.

TRUE FOR ME

I am a new creation (2 CORINTHIANS 5:17).

I am His workmanship (EPHESIANS 2:10).

I am not condemned (ROMANS 8:1).

I am a child of God (JOHN 1:12).

I am a friend of God (JOHN 15:15).

I have been crucified with Christ (GALATIANS 2:20).

I do not have a spirit of fear but of power (2 TIMOTHY 1:7).

I have been chosen by God (COLOSSIANS 3:12).

I have been justified by faith (ROMANS 5:1).

4

Labels Hurt

In junior high and into my first years of high school, I could still ride a bike, go swimming, jump off the diving board, and act like a normal kid. My athletic inability didn't come on full display until running was required. It wasn't that I couldn't catch or hit the ball. I just couldn't run.

And because I couldn't run, I had a label.

I was *that* kid.

Being labeled at such a young age isn't easy to get over. I was the one whose name got met with an audible groan when the other players found out I'd been chosen for their team. When I'd go up to bat I'd hear, "Get the hourglass out. Roozeboom's up to bat." "Roozeboom, were you running? Looks like you're in slow motion. I think you walk faster than you run." "Pinch runner for Roozeboom." Some of the comments might have been under their breath, but I could still hear them.

Labels hurt. There's no doubt about it. And our culture is full of them, words that should be dropped from our vocabulary—loser, retarded, homeless, learning disabled, and my least favorite: handicapped. The list of damaging cultural labels goes on

57

and on, trapping innocent victims in their confining grip. We are all human beings with our own challenges, and not one of us should be reduced to a hurtful label. The most dangerous labels can cause a person to go into a darkness that doesn't seem to end, making them feel there is no hope. Has that happened to you? A teacher calls you unteachable, stupid, making you afraid to try to learn new things; a parent accuses you of being hopelessly lazy, and you believe it, cutting yourself short of all the possibilities you might enjoy if you were only a hard worker; a spouse trades you in for a "newer model," leaving you to question your own self-worth. The collateral damage caused by cultural labels is as unending as the labels.

Some of my classmates called me a loser and a cripple, and I believed them. Being an undesirable cripple sealed the fate of my *that* kid label. I strived to defeat the label by trying even harder. My junior high coach once told my parents, "No one will ever push Rob harder than he pushes himself. But he just can't do it. He can't will it to where he'll be a stud on the field, no matter how much he wants it." The coach knew I had the heart. I just couldn't make my body match it. I felt like a worthless waste of space.

It wasn't only the name calling or snide comments that hurt; it was also the looks I'd get as I walked by, the judgments others made without ever knowing me.

This still happens to me as an adult, unfortunately. My good friend Jay and I were on the road a while back. We made plans to meet an old friend of Jay's for dinner at a hotel restaurant. I wheeled in my wheelchair to join them at the table. We got to talking and Jay's friend, whom I'd never met before, made a strange comment: "Well, you know, everyone in here thinks they're paying for you."

What? You've got to be kidding me. Did this guy seriously assume that just because I was in a wheelchair, I couldn't have a full-time job or a career? That I wasn't man enough to cover the cost of my own meal? That I was a burden to society? What I heard in his comment was a vicious lie, but in that moment it felt dangerously real. The lie screamed in my head, and the label "I'm a burden" sank into my heart—a label slapped on me by a guy I had never met before.

As a kid, I had desperately wanted the label of athlete, jock, a superstar who stood out above the rest. I wanted to be the star quarterback. The game-winning, last-shot-taking, slam-dunk-at-the-buzzer stud. The guy who gained attention just by walking in the room.

Oh, I did accomplish that last goal.

You'd notice when I walked into a room, all right. I had this special, unique swagger about me. A sway that made me look confident. I'm trying to make it sound cool, but it wasn't. It was an awkward strut.

I wish I could say I invented it, but I've seen others walk that way. We kind of have a club. But not everybody can join. There are some common factors you need to join the muscular dystrophy club. However, it doesn't matter your age, your economic background, your social status, your ethnicity, because the factors don't discriminate. That's what makes this club unique. MD will affect each person in its own way, but it will invariably affect them. And the world will notice because we stand out. But again, it's not the athletic stud kind of standing out. It's more the butt of every joke, not quite right, odd-looking kind of standing out.

Our club members have been handed a permanent label. We are called disabled, handicapped, different, and special (but not in a good way). And here's the thing. There is a reality to our condition that is true. Members of the MD club do not have the same physical strength and abilities as a healthy individual. Yet, we have the same brain, heart, soul, ambitions, desires, and heartaches as the rest of humanity.

As followers of Jesus, we need to be mindful of the labels we assign to ourselves as well as to others. Do you know where a damaging label comes from? A lie. In the previous chapter we looked at how destructive lies can be. Those same lies can turn into labels if we let them, and these labels have the power to shape our identity.

Labels Establish Identity

When you are labeled, fear often creeps in and whispers, "They see your inadequacies." This is followed by thoughts like, *I'm not good enough. I'm less than. I'm worthless. I don't belong here. I'm unloved. I'm unvalued. I'm forgotten.*

These lies paralyze us in fear, allowing the label to take root inside us and shape our identity. What we believe about ourselves, we become. Not good enough? No use in attempting to get any better, then, we tell ourselves. So we remain half-baked in our efforts. Worthless? No sense in standing up for ourselves, right? Why bother? So we hide in the shadows, staying out of the way of the more worthy. Forgotten? Then why even try to keep in touch with loved ones or think about anyone besides ourselves? We become isolated human beings when we let that label shape us. Lies form the label, and the label reinforces the lies. What a destructive cycle.

The fear of being stamped with an unfavorable label threatens to prevent us from becoming all that God intends us to become. Instead of embracing the unique creations we are, we fight it. We do everything we can to remain incognito. If you've ever been caught up in this senseless cycle of letting the labels dictate who you are, you're not alone. I have too.

Many smart, capable people get slapped with labels that they try to shy away from. Like the socially awkward nerd, the introvert who is judged for being reclusive, the detail-oriented techy, the dictator-type control freak who has strong leadership skills but hasn't learned to use them yet—you name it. Anyone can get made fun of, even someone with a hobby that may seem odd to others. I mean, not everyone is into chainsaw wood carving, but who cares? These "labels" are actually badges of honor in some cases, even turning into medals later in life: when the nerd works for Google and makes big bucks, the band geek plays in a hot band with a top label, the introvert becomes a respected counselor, and the dictator learns to lead and becomes a respected CEO. You get the idea. There is a redemptive side of the labels, an upside to what was intended to take us down. Instead of shying away from the labels, consider flipping them on their ear and turning them into a strength. Remember, what the Enemy does to harm us, God can use to help not only us but others also. We can take those labels, embrace the parts we choose to, and let them develop into something greater than we can imagine. It took me a long time to learn how to do that, and my deepest hope is that you will not let the labels keep you hogtied like they did me.

I spent years and years trying to be incognito, to blend in, trying to look like everyone else. Pushing back on the fear of my label making me stand out. Saying no to opportunities because I didn't want to be noticed as "special." I let the fear of standing out keep me up at night agonizing over my label, coming up with excuses for why I wouldn't do a certain activity or go to an event because, if I did, I'd have to admit that I fit the label.

More than the pain of being labeled, my muscles were wasting away, and there wasn't a thing I could do about it. The progression of the disease was so emotionally painful. As the disease progressed during my teen years, it became harder and harder to fly under the radar and be "normal." I wanted out of the MD club. It wasn't a club I'd signed up for or wanted to join.

The pain was too intense. I tried to numb it with alcohol. In those later years of high school I got drunk every weekend, starting on Thursday nights. It got scary at times. One night I thought I was going to die because I was so far gone. My friends left me at my car, and I had to find my way home. Today I know how dumb that was. I don't ever want to get drunk again, and I have no need to.

But by the time I reached my senior year of high school, I'd had it. More than once, I drove my car at ninety miles per hour toward a bridge. *This is it. I can drive off that bridge. It will look like an accident, and my pain will be over.* But at the last second I always turned away.

I could turn away from the bridge, but the pain stayed with me. I understand what it is to feel so dark that you don't know what the answer is. I understand that the pain can become so intense you don't want to be here anymore. Trust me, my friend, I know what it's like to have no hope.

Have you lost hope? Are you detouring to get away from the pain, numbing it with alcohol like I did? Or with some other escape like marijuana or mindless social media binging? Working extra-long hours so you don't have to think about it? I get it. Hopelessness causes us to look for ways to numb the pain of the labels. Let me tell you right now, there is hope. And it's not found in any of those temporary modes of escape. We're not trapped inside any label. What I mean is, the labels that get slapped on us, or that we internalize, don't have the power to make us someone we're not. Feeling the persuasive weight of a label isn't the end of the road; it's only part of the journey. Don't give in to the false power that labels try to have over you.

For years, I allowed the cultural labels of disabled, damaged, less-than, to shape me. The voices that had made a rude comment or sometimes yelled idiotic things at me like "Where'd you get that strut?" had more authority on my life than God did. I cared what people thought about me. Their opinions mattered to me more than the opinion of the Creator of the universe, the one who made me in the first place. This is all kinds of screwed up when you think about it. God's Word has so much to say about who we are in His eyes, yet how many of us still put more weight on others' words than God's? That was definitely me. I had a teacher once watch me walk down the hall. Then he yelled out at me, "Boy, you must be one cocky guy to walk like that." I ignored him, but I couldn't ignore how much his ignorant remark hurt. His comment fueled my belief in the cultural label I'd been trying to ignore. I already felt damaged, and in my mind, that made me inferior to my classmates who could parade down the hall like a normal person. I couldn't see a teacher's mistake or God's view of me. All I could see was the label of handicapped (aka broken). The Enemy was winning the battle.

You might be in the battle right now, but don't lose hope. Once we realize we've allowed the Enemy's lies to deceive us and that the cultural labels assigned to us aren't true, we have taken the first step toward overcoming the lies of the label.

Changing Cultural Labels to Spiritual Labels

The world labels us one way. Our label in the world's eyes might be burden, disabled, needy, crippled, handicapped. Or we might feel the weight of an ugly label that calls us a failure, loser, coward, hopeless addict, unwanted, an unlovable not-worth-choosing inferior member of the human race . . . need I say more? There are so many hopeless labels we can get stuck in, like sinking sand that sucks us down until we lose all hope of ever rising above its power.

But God transforms our cultural labels—He changes them to labels that reflect His truth, and that's what He wants for each of us. In God's eyes, we are His children, beloved, forgiven, worthy because of the work of Jesus on the cross, valued, seen, and known. God created each one of us with a purpose. He has intentions for us, plans for who we will become when we place our trust in Him. He designed every individual as a unique creation with specific talents.

Our true help comes when we understand God's label for us. I'm not saying it's easy, but it is possible to replace cultural labels with spiritual labels from God's Word.

From I'm Damaged to I Can Face All Things through Christ

The world tells me I am disabled, handicapped. I despise those labels. Whenever Kory, one of my friends who helps me, pulls us into a handicapped parking space, I tell him to "Put up the Handicrapper sticker." But you know what label I dislike even more? The trendier way of trying to make people like me feel better by calling us "differently abled" instead of disabled. Actually, "kindly" changing the label makes me feel worse. The message I've received is I'm not okay; I'm damaged, still not good enough; that's why the label needs to be changed.

By adjusting the labels to make them more compassionate or more politically correct, we're trying to make life fair. It's not. Telling me I'm differently abled does not change the fact someone has to lift me out of the car. I wish I could walk, not roll, but that's the harsh reality of my life. Some of us are born with a skin color that may make it easier to go most places without being watched with suspicion. Others aren't. And what about legitimate intellectual disabilities? There are those who believe (wish, in my opinion) every person could live independently. But how do you make the playing field level for the person who is severely autistic or someone who has suffered an injury that leaves them unable to mentally function like they did before? Life isn't fair. Changing cultural labels isn't going to change that. I see the idea of changing cultural labels to be more accepting as an attempt at trying to make the playing field level. But we can't simply design a new label, wrap it up and put a bow on it, and expect everything to be level. As much as we may want to believe we can do that, in a broken world, a level playing field can't ever be created.

All of us can relate to this in our own way. Each of us has our own limitations—things we have and don't have, things we can do and things we can't. And for many of us, a deeper, painful label takes root in us, whether we agree with society's labels or not. We feel damaged. Not quite made right. Like we can't pull it together because of some hidden flaw rooted like crabgrass inside us.

And then the Bible tells us we are fearfully and wonderfully made. "I praise you because I am fearfully and wonderfully made; your works are wonderful, I know that full well" (Psalm 139:14 NIV). What a contradiction. One involves limits (disabled, damaged), not being able to do as much, whether physically, mentally, emotionally, socially or whatever. The other describes inspiration, delight, pleasure, admiration, being extremely good. Which label do we listen to?

This reminds me of an old legend. No one is really sure where it originated from, but the meaning of it speaks loud and clear. Allegedly, the story is about a conversation between an elderly Native American grandfather and his grandson. It goes something like this:

An old chief is teaching his young grandson about life.

"A fight is going on inside me," he says to the boy. "It is a terrible fight between two wolves. One wolf is evil and the other wolf is good. The evil wolf is all of the bad inside me—greed, selfishness, lies, anger, envy, arrogance. The other wolf is all that is good within me—love, truth, generosity, humility, patience, wisdom."

As the boy listens carefully, the old man continues. "The same fight is going on inside you, my son, and inside every other person who walks the soil of this great earth."

The grandson thinks about this for a few moments, imagining the good and evil wolves fighting inside his chest. He turns to his grandfather, a concerned look on his young face. "But, Grandfather, which wolf will win?

The wise chief simply replies, "The one you feed."

For too long, I was feeding the wrong wolf. In my pain and resentment, I nurtured the evil label. Damaged beyond repair. Perhaps you have too. We lock ourselves into feeling unlovable and unworthy by focusing on that part of ourselves. I licked my wounds from the bad wolf's attacks that made me feel "less than" because of being physically damaged. I spent far too much time letting the bad wolf overpower the good wolf, allowing the cultural labels to drown out the spiritual labels. Maybe it's because I didn't fully understand the Scripture and its context.

"Fearfully and wonderfully made." It's taken me some time to wrap my brain cells around that one. I think what used to trip me up with this concept is that I was looking at how I was made through a cultural label. We reward the strong and healthy, and we admire athleticism and physical strength. Childhood heroes are fierce knights slaying dragons or brave firemen rescuing babies from upstairs windows. And they're always handsome. Always.

God has made it very clear outward appearance doesn't carry much weight with Him. When it came time to look for a replacement for King Saul, God sent Samuel with specific instructions: "Don't judge by his appearance or height . . . The LORD doesn't see things the way you see them. People judge by outward appearance, but the LORD looks at the heart" (1 Samuel 16:7). Even Jesus apparently wasn't much to look at, and He suffered rejection like none other. The prophet Isaiah described Him in advance. "There was nothing beautiful or majestic about his appearance, nothing to attract us to him. He was despised and rejected—a man of sorrows, acquainted with deepest grief" (Isaiah 53:2–3). I don't dare put myself in the same caliber as Jesus, but I do know what it feels like to be despised and rejected. I've also felt sorrow and grief. I can imagine you have too. Yet Jesus had the purest heart ever, and the heart is what's most important to Him.

One has only to look at beautiful people like Joni Eareckson Tada to see this truth play out in today's world. After becoming a quadriplegic from a diving accident as a teenager in 1967, Joni refused to let cultural labels defeat her. She has been an inspirational example to not only those with similar limitations but to people from all backgrounds. Her artwork (which involves holding a paintbrush with her mouth), singing, message, and ministry have risen above many whom our culture would deem more worthy based on physical stature alone. Hats off to you, Joni!

There are many other examples of God's favor on those whom culture often views as "less than." Have you ever seen the unconditional love in the eyes of a Down syndrome child? Played online chess with a brilliant man with cerebral palsy who has to use a joystick to make his moves? If you have, I bet you lost. I happen to know of a stunning first-grade teacher named Miss J who is in her thirties and in a wheelchair. She has a waiting list of parents who sign up their kids to be in her class because she is such an amazing teacher. The list goes on and on, courageous individuals who refuse to let cultural boundaries defeat them.

I believe this is what the rest of Psalm 139:14 (NIV) is talking about: "Your works are wonderful, I know that full well." I've seen it time and time again. Although the playing field will never be level, the foot of the cross is. Jesus opens His arms to each of us, regardless of our damage or limitations.

Let's look at another story. This one isn't legend. It comes directly from the Bible. The boy's name is Mephibosheth, and he is the son of Jonathan, grandson of King Saul. When Mephibosheth is only five years old, his dad and granddad are killed in battle. Afraid for their lives, Mephibosheth's nurse picks him up and flees. During the hurried escape, Mephibosheth falls and severely injures his legs. In today's terms, he becomes permanently disabled (see 2 Samuel 4:4).

After a difficult childhood of isolation (because no one wants to see the crippled son of a dead king), God redeems the life of this "special" boy. King David, who becomes king after Saul dies, had been close friends with Mephibosheth's father, Jonathan. When he learns that his best friend has a disabled son, King David has the young man brought to the palace to live in a place of honor beside him.

And you know what Mephibosheth says when he first sees the new king? He calls himself a "dead dog," unworthy of the king's kindness (see 2 Samuel 9:8). What a dead-end label. That's not the label God wanted this wounded young prince to have. God had opened David's heart to welcome Mephibosheth into a life of royalty. And for a time, that's what happened. Sadly, the bad wolf kept Jonathan's son trapped inside his destructive label, causing him to lose favor with the very man who offered him a home filled with love. Even though Mephibosheth ended up leaving David's side, David never turned his back on him, even saving him from being executed later in his life. It's quite a remarkable, yet tragic story. You can read the whole thing in 2 Samuel.[1] If only Mephibosheth could have seen God's spiritual label, which offered a better life of being wanted, welcomed, and loved. But he let the cultural label destroy his life. I don't want to miss out on any of the goodness God has planned for my life, do you?

We can learn to overcome the labels' hold on us, but some logistical shortcomings remain. They're unavoidable. So many times I have heard people spout Philippians 4:13 as if it has some kind of superpower. "For I can do everything through Christ, who gives me strength." Some versions say "all things." And I have argued against it in my own mind.

No, I can't. I can't do everything. And that is true. I can't pick up my kids and hug them. I can no longer climb the stairs. I can't get out of this chair I'm sitting in right now without help. Those are some quite legitimate "I can'ts."

Does that make me less of Christian because I can't do this or that? Am I not trusting Christ enough? Why does He not strengthen me that way?

Have you ever been there? Wondering why others seem to be able to do "all things" or "everything" and you can't?

I wrestled with that verse for a long time. I finally gave in, assuming it just meant I could only do certain things, limited things, through Christ who gives me strength—like pray for someone, get up in front of a crowd and speak, lead a Bible study, or other Christian-type things. Not everything or all things. So, it was very confusing to me . . . until I heard it translated more accurately.

The original word for "do" in this context can be better translated as "face," as in confront, meet head-on, square off with, or come to grips with. It doesn't mean you can "do all things or everything"; it means you can "face" all things through Christ who gives you strength. When Paul said he could "do all things," he was referring to dealing with hunger and poor living conditions. He said, "I have learned the secret of living in every situation, whether it is with a full stomach or empty, with plenty or little" (Philippians 4:12). He wasn't saying he could cook up dinner out of thin air. His words were meant to encourage his followers that God will give us the strength to face whatever situations we find ourselves in, good or bad. That makes a whole lot more sense, as far as I'm concerned. I've had countless experiences seeing this one through, facing an obstacle with God-given courage and reaching an acceptance of my limitations. All with God's strength.

Facing the labels head-on along with the disappointment, hurt, confusion, and loss that come with them is possible through Christ who gives us strength. When the world says it's not possible, God says, "Oh yes, it is! It just might not look the way you think."

From I'm Labeled to I'm Set Apart

I don't like being labeled.

The cultural label says "different," but the Bible says "set apart." I love the definition of *set apart*: "to keep something for a special purpose."[2] I had no idea when my childhood dreams were falling apart that God was setting me apart for His purpose. Starting a ministry and speaking in front of thousands of people would have never crossed my mind. Yet, that's what God had planned for me. What might He have you set apart for? If you don't know yet, don't despair. His timing is right, and His plans can't be stopped when we are walking in His will.

When you meet Jesus and welcome Him into your heart, He sets you apart with a fresh set of plans. The Bible says it like this, "This means that anyone who belongs to Christ has become a new person. The old life is gone; a new life has begun!" (2 Corinthians 5:17). Now, that's a different I want!

We gain strength to overcome cultural labels and protection from the bad wolf when we give our lives to Jesus. He sets us apart, but He doesn't leave us hanging. One day while Jesus was having a heart-to-heart with His disciples, He looked toward heaven and prayed for them and for all believers, which includes us. He asked God to protect us and fill us with His truth—truth to see ourselves the way God sees us. "My prayer is not that you take them out of the world but that you protect them from the evil one. They are not of the world, even as I am not of it. Sanctify them by the truth; your word is truth" (John 17:15–17 NIV). I like the way Jesus thinks. In Him, we are set apart and feeding the good wolf.

From I'm a Nobody to I'm a Chosen Child of God

I have a confession to make. Getting the label "I'm a nobody" out of my head has not been easy. I'm a striver, a doer, one who thinks there's something important about accomplishments. And when I can't do something as simple as dress myself, I start to feel like a nobody.

And when I put that into a spiritual perspective, it gets just as complicated. I think I need to accomplish tons of good things for God so He will love me, so He will see I'm a somebody. Yet that's not the message of the cross at all. As my dad has told me over and over, "You'll never earn your way to heaven. You can't do enough good to outweigh the bad." I don't think Dad was telling me that because I'd done so many outrageously bad things. The truth is we don't become somebody because of what we've done for the kingdom of God. We're somebody because of what God has already done for us. We can't earn it, and we sure can't take any credit for it.

These words from Paul help my mind and heart to understand I'm not a nobody: "God saved you by his grace when you believed. And you can't take credit for this; it is a gift from God. Salvation is not a reward for the good things we have done, so none of us can boast about it. For we are God's masterpiece. He has created us anew in Christ Jesus, so we can do the good things he planned for us long ago" (Ephesians 2:8–10).

I'm a somebody because I am a chosen child of God! You are too. Although we are broken, we are still chosen. Listen to these words found in John's account of Jesus' activity on earth: "For this is how God loved the world: He gave his one and only Son, so that everyone who believes in him will not perish but have eternal life" (John 3:16). Being chosen by God isn't about works or earning your way; it's simply about believing in His Son, Jesus.

From I'm a Slave to My Reality to I'm a Co-Heir with Christ

What's just as remarkable is what happens as you become a child of God. I felt the world's labels prohibiting me from amounting to anything, trapped in the hopeless feeling of being a slave to my reality. When our middle daughter, Riley, was about six years old, she was riding on my lap in my wheelchair one night and asked me, "Daddy when will your muscles come back?"

"Why?"

"Because when they do, then you can be a real man and drive a pickup."

Even my little girl believed you amount to something by what you can do; in her mind it was driving a pickup truck. Beliefs like these form the kind of cultural labels that society slaps on us.

For me, I hear these kinds of jabs: "Look at you, you can't do something as simple as walking. You can't do the simplest things in life; how will you ever amount to anything?" These lies make me feel trapped, enslaved to a frightening future. What kind of jabs do you hear, my friend? That someone else can do it better? That you don't have what it takes? That you'll never make it, so you may as well give up now? That's what the enemy wants you to believe.

My beautiful wife, Sharla, continually tells me, "It doesn't matter what you do, it matters who you are!" Who am I? I am a child of God. And the Bible tells me that because of that I'm a co-heir with Christ. Sounds cool. But what does that even mean?

It means no matter how much you feel like a slave to your limited abilities, whether physical, mental, or emotional, on this earth, it doesn't really matter because there is an inheritance waiting for you in heaven. This is true for all who have become children of God. "For all who are led by the Spirit of God are children of God. So you have not received a spirit that makes you *fearful slaves*. Instead, you received God's Spirit when he adopted you as his own children. Now we call him, 'Abba, Father.' For his Spirit joins with our spirit to affirm that we are God's children. And since we are his children, we are his heirs. In fact, together with Christ we are heirs of God's glory" (Romans 8:14–17, emphasis mine).

The rest of verse seventeen says, "But if we are to share his glory, we must also share his suffering." We don't like that part as much, do we? If we've followed Jesus for any amount of time, we can testify to its truth. Labels hurt, especially when you're given them without being asked.

But in glorious reality, any label other than the one God gives you is not your identity! God has given all who believe spiritual labels that far better describe our identity in Him—conqueror, set apart, chosen child of God, co-heirs with Christ, beloved, seen, and not forgotten. Now that's something to celebrate, right? What was so ugly becomes beautiful when we see who we are because of whose we are: chosen children of God.

PRAYER

Lord Jesus, give me the strength and belief to realize my true labels. Help me to let go of labels that were given to me years ago or yesterday. Let me not dwell on them or allow them to take away joy in my life anymore. Help me to replace cultural labels with biblical ones. I'm grateful that my true label is not what the world sees, but what you see. Help me to see who you see—a forgiven, chosen child of God.

In your precious name, Jesus,
Amen.

TRUE FOR ME

I am called (EPHESIANS 4:1).

I am a citizen of heaven (PHILIPPIANS 3:20).

I am a co-heir with Christ (ROMANS 8:15–17).

I have received the Spirit of God (1 CORINTHIANS 2:12).

I have been sanctified through Christ (HEBREWS 10:14; 1 CORINTHIANS 1:30; 1 CORINTHIANS 6:11).

I have been saved by grace (EPHESIANS 2:8–9).

I am set apart (1 PETER 2:9–10).

I am a dearly loved child of God (EPHESIANS 5:1).

5

Learning to Grieve so We Can Heal

Friend, what brokenness are you suffering? Maybe it's a broken marriage. Or the hopeless fear of financial distress. A desperate attempt to have children. A failed career. Kids heading toward disaster. Betrayed friendship. Lonely singleness. Broken dreams. You fill in the blank. Each one of us suffers brokenness in one way or another. Death, betrayal, failure, disappointment. All forms of brokenness represent loss—the loss of something or someone. And on the heel of all brokenness comes grief. Ready or not, here it comes.

Most of us are familiar with the commonly understood stages of grief: denial, anger, bargaining, depression, acceptance—not necessarily in that order or even one at a time. There are many teachings about grief, so I'm not going to explain them all here; I just want to assure you we've all been there in one way or another, sometimes grieving over and over again about the persistent brokenness in our lives. Grieving is not one and done.

I wish going through grief was like a formula: "It hurt" plus "I worked through it" equals "now I'm all better." Wouldn't that be great? Yeah, I haven't been able to do that either. Thankfully, I can say I have been able to grieve certain things less than I once did. But with a disease that seems to take more than it gives, I often find myself grieving the last thing I recently lost physically. And I get to work through the process of grief all over again.

This can also happen for us in work, relationships, health, finances, even getting older. The struggle is real. The grief that accompanies any kind of brokenness is painful.

Because of our heart to help people who are struggling and feel broken, we have a program at RiseFest called Bless A Family (BAF). It's one of my favorite parts of the festival. We started BAF a few years ago to bring comfort and help to weary parents who are walking through adversity. In most cases, sadly, these parents have a child with cancer. Our desire is to help these families understand they are not alone on their painful journey.

Participants of Bless A Family are nominated by friends or family. They are given tickets and a special experience at the festival, like a full tour of the festival grounds and going backstage to meet most of the artists, which I think is exciting. But what I value most is how we love on them by providing a care team to give the exhausted parents a hand with their kids. A team member hangs with the kids so the parents can watch a concert uninterrupted, have a hand at meals, or take a nap. Whatever the family needs, our team is there to Bless A Family!

Not long ago, we added RISE Heroes to our ministry. Our Heroes are adults, often parents themselves, who are fighting cancer or going through other difficult circumstances. One of our recent Heroes, a young newlywed, lost her husband in an accident earlier in the year. We were able to give her and her extended family a specialized experience at RiseFest, offering comforting attention so she wouldn't feel so alone.

I always get to meet our Bless A Family, but my heart's desire is to also meet all our RISE Heroes. What's really special is when we get the opportunity to pray with the Heroes. When the weekend comes to an end, the families will return home and their difficult trials will still be there. We hope the positive memories from RiseFest will provide a bright spot in their day, because no one knows what tomorrow holds.

For each family, we remain hopeful for recovery, but that doesn't always happen. We've walked with families who have celebrated the cancer going into remission as well as those whose loved one went to be with Jesus. We grieve alongside each family in their loss. Our friendship with BAF families and Heroes extends beyond the festival weekend. We walk alongside them all year long where we can.

I completely understand that grief doesn't simply go away just because someone did a nice deed for you. Grief is persistent. But so is Christ's love. It is important to us at RISE Ministries to continue providing hope for these grieving families and individuals throughout the year, to remind them of God's constant love. Because His love doesn't show up for a music-filled weekend once a year and then withdraw into hiding for the next twelve months. His love for us is constant, regardless of whether we can feel it or not. And let's be honest. When we're grieving, we don't usually feel all warm and fuzzy. Grief can stop good feelings in their tracks, overpowering them with anger and despair, confusion and loneliness. And yet . . . God loves each of us with an unconditional love that understands the depth of our grief. Each of us can take comfort in that truth. If your grief threatens to overwhelm you today, I want to encourage you, friend. The same love and hope our BAF and RISE Heroes receive from Jesus is available to you as well. In the middle of your grief, or in the beginning, when you first receive the devastating news, or at the tail end of your healing journey, He is there for you.

You Can Have Hope in the Middle of Grief

Sharla, our kids, and I became extra close friends to one BAF family in particular. Their son, Tripp, who was the same age as our youngest daughter, was diagnosed at age nine with brain cancer. During Tripp's cancer battle, our families enjoyed dinners together, went boating, shared laughs and tears.

When I met Tripp and his family, he had been battling cancer for quite a few years and was into his treatment. One evening when my son Jager and I were visiting, Tripp was going to play baseball with his buddies. He invited Jager and me along. The side effects of treatment were evident on Tripp's body, but his fighting spirit allowed him to still swing the bat and make his way down the first base line.

Then Tripp challenged me to hit the ball.

There was no way. "I haven't hit the ball in a long time, Tripp."

"You can do it. I know you can," said Tripp. His faith was big. And not just in the hard things, but in God.

My inner pep talk began. *How am I going to let the kid fighting cancer call me out? Come on, Rob. Get up there and make a fool of yourself. You can't wuss out on Tripp.* So, I pulled up to the plate in my wheelchair, picked up a bat I could swing, and eyed up the twelve-year-old pitcher as I waited for the ball to come in. And then . . . *bam!* On the first pitch I hit it out of the park! Just kidding . . . I swung, and then I swung again, and again, and again. I think I got eight to ten strikes (family rules) and then finally I hit the ball. I pushed the joystick on my wheelchair as hard as I could, trying to beat the throw from the infield.

"Safe!"

To my surprise, I made it safely to first base. The next team member at bat hit the ball into the outfield, and I wheeled all the way around the bases, crossed home plate, and scored a point for my team. I'd forgotten how good that felt.

Tripp was my biggest cheerleader. "I knew you could do it!" His belief in me was as big as his smile.

When I heard the news that there was no more treatment for Tripp, my heart broke. I couldn't imagine the grief his parents, Chad and Maria, and Tripp's brother, Caleb, were going to experience. To make matters worse, before Tripp breathed his last breath on earth, his grandfather, Chad's dad, died in an accident as he was cutting a tree in his backyard.

After the accident, I sat with Chad as he shared with me his continued faith in God. There we sat, two friends, brothers in Christ, as Chad declared that God is good and loving, even in pain and grief.

I wanted to scream for him! *But why, God? Why?! My friend's son is fighting a cancer battle that seems terminal and now you've taken his dad as well? What's up with that?!* I couldn't bring myself to accept God's goodness. Grief had me tied up in knots.

Yet through all of their grief, my friends held on to their hope and their love for God. Especially Tripp. Tripp's attitude and faith through it all inspired me on my own journey of loss and frustration. It came through a casual interview with Tripp and his pastor. The pastor asked, "What do you want others to know?" Without hesitation Tripp answered, "How good God is!"

I still have a lump in my throat as I write this. At the time I couldn't fathom what he was saying. *Tripp, how can you say that? You're dying. You have fought over and over through treatments. And what you loved—sports—you lost, just like me. Your body won't let you participate in life anymore, just like me . . . and you want to tell everyone how good God is?* Tripp's brokenness came in the form of cancer. My brokenness at the time was a struggle with faith.

This young man taught me so much about pain and loss, about hope and life. I don't like being in a chair, and I often wonder, *God, where have you gone?* Tripp taught me to look for the goodness of God in the pain. He taught me that there can still be joy in loss, that you can still add joy to others' lives in the midst of grief. Even in the hospital, he made doctors and nurses laugh. Knowing no stranger, Tripp was never afraid to talk about his faith. For a kid who knew his time was short, he loved pointing people to Jesus. He was so excited to go see his grandpa, priding himself in being the first one to see him in heaven. After a five-year battle with cancer, Tripp went to be with Jesus in 2022. He was only fourteen years old.

Tripp lived with the mentality that this life isn't all there is, this world is not our home, and that God's goodness outlasts grief. I want to live with that mentality, as hard as it is.

Yes, God is good. Yet, that truth doesn't take away the grief of parents whose son went to heaven way too soon. And it doesn't take away the grief of my situation or yours. Grief is an unavoidable part of being human. When we think of grief, we most often picture it following the death of a loved one. That's what I used to think: *You only grieve when someone you love dies.* I've long since learned death isn't the only loss that causes grief. There's more. Grief comes with being broken. When we are broken, we grieve misplaced expectations, disappointments, losing what once was or what will most likely never be.

Everyone's Brokenness Is Different, but Grief Is the Same

My friend Kory travels with me quite often, and we end up having some good conversations. As he was helping me one day, I asked him, "If you had a breakout session on being 'broken still chosen,' what would it be?"

It didn't take him long to come up with his answer. "Everyone's brokenness is different, but grief and pain are the same."

He's so right. Everyone's brokenness is specific to that person, but grief and pain stab our hearts the same. Although your brokenness may be different from mine, we both feel the unavoidable pain that comes with the grief of being broken.

Brokenness is not exactly the same for any two people, even if the circumstances are similar, because no two people are the same. Even fellow members of the muscular dystrophy club are broken in other ways. In addition to physical limitations with MD, we experience broken relationships, inner doubts, fears of the future, and constant disappointment that our lives aren't what we think they should be. I'm quite certain we're not the only ones, right?

Brokenness shows up in so many shapes and forms. For years Kory had the dream of trucking together with his son, until his son died in a trucking accident at eighteen years old. Kory lost his son and his dream. I can no longer move my major muscles, confining me to a life of consistent need for care and constant need to renew my faith. Different brokenness, same grief.

Grief Is Necessary for Healing and Wholeness

What if I told you there is a surprising flipside to grief? Whenever we experience loss, it becomes necessary for grief to be involved so we can experience wholeness. Grief has a purpose. It took me a while to learn that lesson. When Tripp went to join his grandpa in heaven, I wanted to sit and stew in my grief, mostly in the anger stage. But God wouldn't let me. Neither would Tripp's parents. Chad and Maria continued to live out their faith in the middle of their hurts, encouraging me to do the same. We had to admit the pain and work through the grief, supporting one another along the way. Same with Kory. And countless others. I learned from John Townsend that when you bring grief to community, it's cut in half.[1] My personal experience has shown me how true that is.

I've walked through a lot of grief, seen and felt a wide spectrum of emotions with the Bless A Family members, RISE Heroes, friends, and family over the years. Sometimes our grief includes downright sobbing, what some of the girls would call an ugly cry. I've been told an ugly cry includes running mascara and lots of tissues. For guys, I'm willing to guess, an ugly cry would include yelling words at God we'd rather the girls not hear. Different brokenness. Same grief.

When we allow ourselves to feel the pain, to embrace the grief, we throw our hearts wide open to the inner places where healing can happen. Grief works like a healing power wash, releasing the crustiness and muck of bitterness so our hearts can heal.

Grieving Is Biblical

If you were raised like I was, you don't show sad emotions. Doing so would reflect weakness, or so we think. But that's not true at all. Quite the contrary, in fact.

Even King David knew the highs and lows of life and the grief of being broken. He kills Goliath as a young man and he's a hero. He's noticed. He becomes a mighty warrior in Saul's army. He becomes best friends with Saul's son, Jonathan, the dad of Mephibosheth. The Israelites start to shout how great David is, fueling a fire within Saul to kill him (see 1 Samuel 17–18). David now is on the run hiding from Saul in caves, and this goes on until Saul's death. When David learns that Saul and Jonathan have died in battle, "David and his men tore their clothes in sorrow when they heard the news" (2 Samuel 1:11). Even the mighty warrior King David was not immune to grief, and he didn't grieve alone. His valiant soldiers tore up their tunics and cried alongside him. Before his firstborn son with Bathsheba died seven days after his birth, David fasted and prayed, lying on the floor, not eating (see 2 Samuel 12:16–18). Later in his life, David ached as news met him that his son, Absalom, had died in battle. "Then the king was very upset, and he went to the room over the city gate and cried. As he went, he cried out, 'My son Absalom, my son Absalom! I wish I had died and not you. Absalom, my son, my son!'" (2 Samuel 18:33 NCV) That kind of sounds like an ugly cry to me. Tissues even.

The idea that we can, or should, hold it all together on our own is not biblical. In the Old Testament, they would call for the wailing women, professional mourners in ancient society to help entire communities learn to grieve. "This is what the LORD Almighty says: 'Consider now! Call for the wailing women to come; send for the most skillful of them'" (Jeremiah 9:17 NIV). I think we sometimes forget that lamenting is a biblical thing. The definition of lamenting is to express sorrow, mourning. We are not the first ones to have ever been hurt or felt the pain of loss. The Old Testament is filled with stories of those expressing great grief and sorrow, crying out to God to hear their cries. The entire book of Lamentations in the Bible was written by a poet who offers five poems of heartache, pain, and suffering, lamenting what once was and asking God to not forget them. Where did we ever get the idea we need to be so stoic? And heaven forbid, ever let anyone else see or share in our grief? Not from the Bible, that's for sure.

After Moses died, Israel mourned his death for thirty days (see Deuteronomy 34:8). As their leader, he led them out of captivity and slavery. He showed them miracles as God parted the Red Sea, provided manna while they were in the desert, and guided them with a cloud by day and a pillar of fire for light by night (see Exodus 13–14). Moses brought down from Mount Sinai the Ten Commandments after God gave them to him (see Exodus 20). Moses played a major role in their lives—their voice from God—and now he was gone. Grief was upon Israel. Grief was real then, and it is real now.

Emotions Are Not Bad

Emotions are going to come out in one of two ways: healthy or unhealthy. The pain is intense at times, depending on the day, but bottling it all up inside doesn't fix anything. The more it gets bottled up, the more the combustion builds. And just like when we shake up a bottle of pop (that's what we call it in Iowa; don't laugh), when the lid comes off, look out! The same is true for our emotions. You and I can try and push them down, say we're going to get over it, keep our eyes from ever shedding a tear in public . . . but it doesn't work forever. Thankfully so. We need to grieve to heal.

When I hold in my emotions too long, I eventually get edgy, agitated, even angry. Sadly, those closest to me take the brunt of it. It's usually not their fault. They were simply in the wrong place at the wrong time when my emotions decided to come out. Guys, tell me I'm not alone in this.

I lost it one time at a youth retreat when I was in high school. One of the fellas was messing around, holding my arms behind my back. I told him to knock it off, but he didn't. When I tripped, he landed on me and pressed my face into the rug. I ended up with a massive rug burn all around my eye. I lost it. For the next thirty minutes I went on a rant; I slammed a friend against the wall, threw a table across the room, and slammed doors. (This was back when I could do this type of physical venting.) All because I hadn't let my emotions come out earlier in a healthy way. I didn't have a counselor; I didn't talk about the grief I was feeling about losing my physical capabilities. I'd just hold it in, all stoic-like, until I couldn't anymore. Then I'd get mad and explode. Not a healthy way to deal with my emotions. Being able to talk to someone or having a community willing to jump in the well of grief with me would have been a much healthier way to do it. A much healthier way for all of us, in fact.

It has taken several years and many vulnerable conversations with trusted friends and counselors to help me learn how to release my emotions in a healthier way. On a not-so-good day, you might hear me yelling in my office. Unless I'm calling for help, no need to check on me. It's all a part of the process of releasing my emotions in a healthier way than ramming my wheelchair into someone's shin. I am grateful for the godly friends God has brought into my life who are willing to let me vent when I need to. And I've become a pretty good listener for them as well. This is what John Townsend was talking about. We cut our grief in half when we share our pain with others. Your emotions are not wrong, and we all have them. Stuffing them isn't the answer.

Processing Brings Healing

There are plenty of ways of dealing with our grief negatively: alcohol, drugs, unhealthy relationships, anger, becoming a workaholic, selfishness, guarding ourselves, becoming short-tempered, distant, building up a wall so high we won't let God in . . . the list could go on and on. All of these short-lived solutions have disastrous endings. Believe me, I understand the desire to drown out grief. I also understand the danger of dealing with grief in such unhealthy ways. The buried or ignored grief doesn't go away, and the unhealthy ways of dealing with it add to your pain.

My friend, there are healthy ways of grieving. Realizing that is so freeing! Having friends who are there for you, who can handle a venting session, or who will sit with you while you shed tears and spill honestly about your hurt, will do wonders in bringing about healing.

Kory and I talk often about our grief and loss. He calls it windshield time. Conversations come up while we spend hours together on the road. Kory is literally helping me with my loss of physical independence as MD continues to take more and more of my muscles every year. I get to remind Kory of God's love for him even though his son is no longer on this earth with us.

If we never process our brokenness with safe friends, the voice in our heads can tell us stories that only add to the hurt and pain. Processing out loud is healing. The more we share our stories and frustrations with trusted listeners, the more healing we find. Especially when we are sharing with others who will process our grief with us, those who are gifted or trained in grief counseling.

It is worth the effort to seek out godly support to help you work through your pain, loss, and grief. If you think you're alone, you're not. I mean, besides having a healthy community where you feel safe to share, God already knows the grief you're carrying. It's okay to vent to our Father, to lay it all out, to speak it, and then leave it in His hands, trusting Him at His word as David shares in Psalm 31:14 (NIV), "But I trust in you, LORD; I say, 'You are my God.'"

Grief and Joy Can Coexist

I've heard it said many times, "God will never give us more than we can handle." I used to believe that, and it confused me because there was so much I couldn't handle. How about you? I'd like to propose a fresh perspective, a more truthful view of that saying, one that settles better with my broken self. It goes like this: "Of course God will give you more than you can handle, because He knows the best thing for us is to depend on Him." That makes a lot more sense, doesn't it? It doesn't matter how spiritually mature, how capable, how strong any of us are, none of us can hold it all together on our own. We need you, God! Remembering the goodness of God will help us when we feel overwhelmed by the grief of our brokenness.

Five days after RiseFest 2022, Sharla and I had traveled to attend a funeral. Taking a simple step in the hotel room with my wife's help, something went wrong. I hit the floor in pain. Rather than going to urgent care, we drove the three-and-a-half-hour trip to see my doctor at home. I hoped the doc would tell me to ice and elevate and I'd be good in a couple of days. Instead I found out I had broken my left foot. I would need to be in a walking boot for at least six to eight weeks. My heart sank. I knew the fate awaiting me. *I'll never walk again if I don't keep doing it now.*

And that's what happened. Eight weeks later the boot came off, and I've not been able to walk like I did before. I can barely take ten steps today with help (I'm not talking on my own). I miss it. I miss it so much, simply walking.

The other night a sense of loss flooded me as I looked at our living room. *Brokenness. Grief.* I thought about what I have lost, not being able to take simple steps into another room. It may sound trivial, but it hurt. To be honest, it still hurts now. When I see people walk, I think, *Walking is a privilege.* (I have to remind a certain daughter of ours that's a true statement.) Something as simple as walking is gone, and that brings tremendous loss into my life. *More than I can handle, Lord.*

And then there's date night. Sharla and I used to love to travel and go to events, but she can't lift me like she used to, so we really have to think about where we're going and if we can make it work. It's not nearly as romantic a dinner out if we have to take a guy along to help me in the men's room. I grieve not being able to have those moments with my wife.

As I write this, I realize I am not the only one grieving these kinds of losses. And even greater ones. You may have lost a spouse completely and want me to stop complaining about not being able to go out on a date with mine. Or you might be able to walk, but your heart is so broken from some other pain that you want only to stay in bed all day long. I hear you. Go ahead and grieve, my friend.

Grief is a necessary part of the healing process. Just don't allow yourself to stay there. Find a friend to process with. Cry out to God. I encourage you to confess to God that what you're going through is more than you can handle. Go ahead and ugly cry. He wants to show us His love for us in those humble times. He reminds us of His goodness when we come before Him in complete honesty, no pretense. He listens. He cares. He comforts. Total openness with God is a healthy way to grieve.

Recently, one area of grief really caught me off guard. I never thought I'd grieve letting our children grow up and leave the nest, but here I am writing about it. Jager has been traveling with me since he was about four years old. As he got older, he became a huge part of helping me physically get around and take some of the pressure off my wife. Jager and I have spent hours on the road together also having windshield time. Many memories pop into my mind as I think about all the places we have been together and the laughs and experiences we've shared. But then he joined the National Guard, did basic training, then went to work for a farmer and run heavy equipment. I miss having him with me every day. I admit it. I am grieving.

The crazy thing I've learned is that both grief and joy can exist at the same time. Joy isn't happiness. It's much deeper than that. Some theologians call joy a spiritual-level happiness. It's that moment when there can be a tear streaming down your face but there's joy in your heart. It's why I can cheer Jager on even though I miss him.

It reminds me of when Jesus tells His disciples that sadness will be turned to joy in John 16. Jesus has spent the last three years with these guys. They've had windshield time (okay, it was more like walking-from-place-to-place time, but you get it). Imagine the memories and ministry the disciples are reflecting on with all their time spent with Jesus. Raising the dead, healing the sick, feeding the crowds fish and bread that won't stop coming, Jesus telling Peter to step out of the boat during the storm and walk on water toward Him. Now Jesus is saying, "You're not going to see me for a while."

I'm not saying my letting go of my son to follow his dreams is the same as what Jesus is about to do and how the disciples are going to react to it. What I'm saying is that even when we grieve, there can be joy.

I can only imagine the thoughts going through the disciples' minds as Jesus tries to prepare them. He says,

> "In a little while you won't see me anymore. But a little while after that, you will see me again."

Some of the disciples asked each other, "What does he mean when he says, 'In a little while you won't see me, but then you will see me,' and 'I am going to the Father'? And what does he mean by 'a little while'? We don't understand."

Jesus realized they wanted to ask him about it, so he said, "Are you asking yourselves what I meant? I said in a little while you won't see me, but a little while after that you will see me again. I tell you the truth, you will weep and mourn over what is going to happen to me, but the world will rejoice. You will grieve, but your grief will suddenly turn to wonderful joy. It will be like a woman suffering the pains of labor. When her child is born, her anguish gives way to joy because she has brought a new baby into the world. So you have sorrow now, but I will see you again; then you will rejoice, and no one can rob you of that joy."

John 16:16–22

Jesus knew the depth of grief His followers would endure. Imagine the grief the disciples must have felt when everything Jesus talked about started happening. Simon Peter sure showed a surge of emotion when he drew his sword to protect Jesus from being arrested. He was in the anger phase. But Jesus also anticipated the indescribable joy they would have once He rose from the dead. Such a contrast of emotions.

Grief is heartache and tears, and it's important to feel, reflect, and express those feelings. If we don't, how will we ever know the joy that Jesus is describing? The joy no one can rob from us. The joy He's talking about comes from the Holy Spirit, a joy that meets us even in the pain. Our joy doesn't come through the avoidance of loss, disappointment, grief, or saying good-bye. It comes from trusting God. It comes from allowing ourselves to admit the pain of grief that our brokenness brings and to surrender that grief to our heavenly Father who understands our hurt, who wants to heal our pain. Jesus promised the disciples that their terrible sorrow would turn to joy. God fulfilled His promise for them, and He will fulfill His promises for us.

Grief has a purpose; it is necessary for healing and wholeness. Grief purges your heart and prepares it for the kind of joy that only Jesus can bring.

PRAYER

Dear Jesus, my heart is heavy today as I grieve for the things that I've lost but also for those who I care deeply about. God, so often I try to suppress my emotions and hide my grief. Help me to know that it's not wrong to feel the feelings and to process them with close, trusted friends. I want the grief to go away, but I know it's a process and that I need you. Remind me you're carrying me and that the Spirit is uttering the words for me when the grief is so great, I can't get them out.
In your powerful, precious name I pray, Jesus.
Amen.

TRUE FOR ME

God comforts me when I mourn (MATTHEW 5:4).

God heals me when I am brokenhearted (PSALM 147:3).

God promises me joy after sorrow (JOHN 16:22).

God blesses me when I recognize my need for Him (MATTHEW 5:3).

God strengthens my heart (PSALM 73:26).

God tells me not to be troubled but to trust Him (JOHN 14:1).

I am healed by His wounds (ISAIAH 53:5).

Jesus understands my grief (ISAIAH 53:3).

Jesus grieves with me (JOHN 11:33–35).

God is with me and tends to my needs (PSALM 23:1–4).

6

Weakness Shows Strength

Before we got married, Sharla and I traveled to visit her sister and brother-in-law in Minnesota. We hadn't been dating long, so this was the first time I'd be meeting them. They didn't know about my diagnosis. I wasn't going around talking about having MD back then; I was trying to secretly fit in the best I could. I'd slowly scale stairs when no one was looking, crawl out of my chair after everyone left the room. I chose to drive a vehicle that was higher off the ground so I could get out of it more easily. In the back of my mind, I still thought (maybe pretended) my diagnosis wasn't as bad as it actually was.

Did I mention we went to Minnesota in the middle of winter? I'm not a fan of the cold even though I am an Iowa boy. I had just returned from Arizona where I'd been for a year and a half after high school graduation. I'm much more a fan of desert winters. Going outside in the winter in Arizona was great; going outside in the land of Minnesota's ten thousand frozen lakes? Not so great.

But I needed a smoke (a bad habit I thankfully quit soon after that). So I bundled up and headed out the back door of Sharla's sister's house into the middle of frigid winter. As I looked up at the night sky, the cold air turning my breath to steam, I slipped and fell in a snowbank. Try as I might, I couldn't climb out of that snowbank by myself. I needed help or I was going to freeze out there. My hopes of blending in were dashed.

My brother-in-law Dave came to the rescue. With his help and the humble swallowing of my pride, I was soon up and out of that deadly snowbank and back in the warm house. Of course, as we sat around the living room while I dried myself in front of the fireplace, the conversation turned to muscular dystrophy—the reason I, as a grown man, could not pull myself out of a two-foot deep snowbank.

After hearing the details of my grim diagnosis, my sister-in-law Shelly fixed her eyes on me. Then she spoke to me and said as bluntly as anyone could say it . . .

"You have MD. So what? Get over it."

Harsh.

She went on to say, "If you wanna go boating, jet skiing, drive a combine, tractor, semi-truck . . . whatever it is, we'll find a way."

I had never had anyone single-handedly dispute all the excuses of living with a disease like mine. It took some brass for her to say that. I was shocked, a little bit ticked. *Who are you to tell me what's possible?* I don't think I said anything to her, but I sure wanted to. *Easy for you to say. You're not living it!*

At the same time, I thought about what she was truly saying. "Come on, Rob. We're going to live life and have fun, and we want you to join us. Don't let MD hold you back."

You have MD. So what? Get over it.

It was the best piece of advice I could get. It was as if she knew I had this attitude of "Tell me I can't, and I'll find a way to prove you wrong." But it would require me learning how to be humble and vulnerable beyond my wildest imagination. For years I'd been attempting to live as though the disease couldn't make me broken. It worked for a while. But the downside of all that pretending was that I was acting like someone I wasn't. I was becoming one of those people I don't like. Fake. Fake people distort reality for their own peace of mind. But it can't last. The real has to come out. Ironically, strength starts to emerge when we at last grab fake by the throat and start to replace it with honest vulnerability.

After Sharla and I were married, I was now surrounded by this attitude of "We'll find a way to do it. No excuses." My vulnerability had been exposed. No more hiding. It was time to be authentic and deal with the serious reality of my life. I know this sounds like an attitude of pull yourself up by your bootstraps, but it's deeper than that. It gets more difficult to pull on any kind of bootstrap as this disease of limb-girdle MD progresses. I have gone from being as active as any little kid on a farm, to a teen playing sports (kind of), to watching almost every piece of independence I once knew fade away. What I'm talking about is facing fear—the fear of looking awkward and feeling the ridicule of strangers, the fear of not being able to do the things you love.

You might know the fear I'm calling out here. For you it might be the fear of being stuck in the wrong career, or not ever finding a spouse who will love you in all of your brokenness, or the fear of not being able to resist the addiction that tempts you constantly. What happens if you confess and you still fail? Yep, that's a scary fear. I know what you're going through.

It's so easy to get caught up in this fear. It's easier to stay where we are familiar, even if it's miserable, instead of taking the courage to tiptoe out of our comfort zone and admit it out loud—I am weak, and I need help.

I'm Not Okay, and That's Okay.

I want to do a lot of things on my own, but they're not going to happen without a miracle. I had to cry out for help when I fell into that snowbank because if too much time passed and no one noticed I was missing, I could have frozen to death. And with the lies of "you're forgotten" still badgering me, spending the night in a snowbank didn't seem too farfetched. For someone else, not being okay might mean getting lured into a bar rather than a snowbank or getting stuck on an inappropriate website or in an ungodly conversation. We all have our areas of weakness that we fight to overcome. The weakness isn't the issue; giving in and letting it win is.

As long as I tried to hide my physical limitations, my pride was keeping me trapped in a false reality where I was missing out on living a full life. My pride declared, "I know I'm lying to myself, but I'm going to do everything on my own to be okay anyway." Not very smart.

There's a deeper truth our weakness says about us. Weakness says, "I'm not okay," and I'm learning that's okay. Authentic vulnerability is not only okay, but also necessary so we can become who God has created us to be. Being open, first to ourselves and God, and then to others, paves the way to reaching an entirely new level of okay. Being okay with our weakness is what moves us toward strength. It takes more strength to be open and honest than to continue to hide behind the excuse of weakness.

And when I say open, I mean full-on vulnerability. I need help with just about everything. I need help dressing, undressing, using the bathroom, getting in and out of the car, showering. There is a difference in how much help I need between local travel and overnight travel. Going to a third world country adds a whole new dynamic. I've been overseas five or six times. In 2006, God allowed me to travel to Bolivia on my first mission trip out of the country. I didn't have a wheelchair or scooter to help me get around at that time. I could walk once someone helped me up. My brother, Bill, got to be the "lucky" guy to go along and be the muscle.

We landed in Cochabamba and got off the plane to see military guys standing guard with machine guns strapped to their backs.

I wondered what they were going to think seeing a guy like me getting carried onto a bus. Looking weak had followed me all the way to Bolivia.

My brother got me up the bus steps and through a second door to our seats. As we finally sat, I told Bill, "This isn't going to work all week." So, the next day we had a vehicle to travel in. Bill had to load me in and out every time. Nothing was very accessible, but we made it work—even on the day we parked at the bottom of a mountain with the school we were to visit up on top. I gazed up at the school, then turned to Bill.

"Well, how are we getting up there?"

"Simple."

He pulled one of my arms around his shoulder and another guy on the trip let me put my other arm around him. Each of them grabbed a leg, and up the mountain we went. The school courtyard was full of kids lined up waiting for our team. I was the first person they saw as I got carried in. For a moment I felt like a rock star as they were all cheering, until I realized they were just happy to see all of us.

My physical weakness had become worse when I went on one of my last overseas trips in 2019. This time I traveled to Haiti with a different team, and my brother wasn't the muscle; my son Jager took the lead on that part. Two of my brothers-in-law and some friends also joined us on the trip. This time, leaving my wheelchair at home wasn't an option. My mobility looked a lot different than it had thirteen years earlier in Bolivia. I needed help with everything.

Every day, the guys on our team stepped in and loaded me, chair and all, into the back of *tap taps*, Haiti's version of taxis. They're actually brightly painted buses or old pickup trucks with metal covers, but they got us where we needed to go. The guys even built me a ramp once we were on sight so I could get into the room Jager and I would be staying in. Needing help was becoming more and more the norm even though I was fighting it.

One day Jager was helping me get from the bathroom to the kitchen to finish up so we could head out.

A frustrated "Ugh" spewed out of me.

"What's wrong with you?" Jager asked.

"I'm so sick of needing help!"

"That's why you got me, Dad." A smile spread across his face.

He caught me off guard with that one. And he was so amazingly right. God had provided me the help I needed—in the coolest roommate ever, my son, and the best teammates who were willing to help however they could. I'm not a big fan of being needy, but I love what we do, and I love to travel. So, it's either ask for help or stay home. And I don't want to stay home. I want to be a part of God's work.

How about you? Is your weakness holding you back from being a part of God's work? I know what it's like to sit alone in the dark with a rope in your hands, broken, unproductive, and lonely because you wouldn't ask for help. In case that's where you are, my friend, let me assure you that the isolation strategy doesn't get you anywhere. If you need help to heal or to overcome a stronghold in your life, the beginning step is simple. Ask for help. That can be as minor as finally sharing your inner struggle with another person. When you let someone else into your story, you never know what incredible things can happen.

Humility Takes Sacrifice

Letting someone else into the inside part of our weakness takes a great deal of humility. There's no question humility is a big deal to God. Humility is referenced in the Bible dozens of times. I'm sure you've heard it said, "Pride goes before destruction, and haughtiness before a fall" (Proverbs 16:18). It's clear God doesn't think very highly of people who think too highly of themselves. Peter talks about this. "God resists the proud, but gives grace to the humble" (1 Peter 5:5 NKJV).

And yet . . .

For so many of us, pride and humility stand off against each other at opposite ends of a persistent tug-of-war. Humility is the opposite of pride. Pride says, "Look at me; look at what I did." Humility says, "Look at them; look at what they did." Humility takes the focus off ourselves and puts it on others. When we are humble instead of being selfish, we become selfless. I'm not saying it's easy. It's not.

Even the disciples struggled with humility. I love the story of Jesus' disciples arguing about who was the greatest. I picture it in my head like a bunch of teenagers arguing over who's the coolest, one-upping each other as they brag about their accomplishments, and Jesus listening, maybe even rolling His eyes because He knows them; I mean *knows* them. Dr. Luke recorded it like this:

> Then they began to argue among themselves about who would be the greatest among them. Jesus told them, "In this world the kings and great men lord it over their people, yet they are called 'friends of the people.' But among you it will be different. Those who are the greatest among you should take the lowest rank, and the leader should be like a servant. Who is more important, the one who sits at the table or the one who serves? The one who sits at the table, of course. But not here! For I am among you as one who serves."
>
> Luke 22:24–27

I bet things got pretty quiet after Jesus spoke. The disciples just got schooled by Jesus. What Jesus is trying to teach these guys is that we grow stronger when we let our weakness keep us humble.

I used to find humility painful. It made me feel "less than" others or who I wish I could be. I know that's messed up, but I already feel "less than" because of my physical brokenness. Adding humility to my limited reality kind of slapped me in the face. In discussing this with a friend one day, he shared something with me that changed the way I have viewed humility from that day on. He said, "It takes sacrifice to be humble." I'd never thought about that before. *Humility takes sacrifice. Hmm.*

To help me understand the fullness of what my friend was saying, I looked up the definition of sacrifice. It means "to suffer loss of, give up, renounce, injure, or destroy especially for an ideal, belief, or end."[1] That's a lot to swallow when you stop and think about it. If humility takes sacrifice, that means when I'm humble, I give up having it all figured out or looking like I have it all together. I give up the right to be right. There has to be a significant trade-off. And that's the point! God prefers the humble; He honors the humble; He gives grace to the humble. Humility is an exchange of pride for grace and honor. I'll make that trade all day long.

Building Stronger Relationships in Our Weakness

Although I'm learning a lot about humility, putting my weakness on full display isn't my favorite thing to do. My most noticeable weakness is physical, and it's taken years for me to let others in to help me with my physical weakness. Being in a wheelchair no longer allows me to hide that weakness. But I can hide others.

Well, I try to hide them anyway. I have kind of earned a reputation of being a fast driver. When people ask me why I drive my car so fast, I answer, "Because I have to do everything else so slow!" With limb-girdle muscular dystrophy, my major muscles closest to my body are the ones that are deteriorating. That means I still have use of my hands and feet. *Hello, steering wheel and gas pedal!* So here you have it in writing: I have a weakness of not obeying the speed limit. My wife would say I have a bigger weakness of not obeying rules, period, but this isn't her book. One day I was speeding down the street in my motorized wheelchair while taking care of emails on my phone. Looking down, I didn't see the pickup truck parked directly in my path with its tailgate down until I slammed right into the back of it. He'd parked in a stupid place, and I was going too stupid fast and not looking where I was going. Two morons in the middle of the street. My wife had no sympathy when I told her about it.

One of my more serious weaknesses is my inability to say no, which causes friction in my marriage and with my kids. I've missed birthdays, anniversaries, and other important events, oftentimes in the name of work. Or, to be honest, I can't say no to social events. The echo I hear in my head right now is: *Rob is not great at boundaries.* I am discovering how to get a better handle on this, however, much through the accountability of good friends and my extra-patient wife. It helps that my inner circle of friends and family knows I stink at boundaries. They are helping me to understand that sometimes we have to say no to good things in order to find great things. Admitting our weaknesses, coming out of hiding, and sharing our brokenness with trusted friends paves the way for us to see growth and victory in our lives.

A friend of mine has a brother who hid his weaknesses, buried them deep, for years. In the public eye he was a local pastor, a husband, and a father to two great kids. In secret, he was a slave to pornography—not a weakness he wanted on full display. He couldn't reveal his sin to anyone for fear of losing his ministry and his family. His weakness prevented him from being able to overcome the addiction; it also kept him isolated, which perpetuated the addiction and the shame. It wasn't until divorce threatened to destroy the family that this struggling pastor finally opened up about his weakness, first with a trusted friend, then with his new support group at Celebrate Recovery. For years since then, he has been meeting with his CR group every week. This dear brother humbled himself and confessed his weakness in a safe place, and now has some of the best friends he's ever had in his life. Oh, and he and his wife are nearing their fiftieth wedding anniversary. All because he chose to make the sacrifice of humility and let others into his weakness.

The Enemy wants to keep us trapped in our weakness, using it to keep us from releasing our full potential. Imagine what would happen if we all stepped into humility and let someone into those weaknesses. Letting others into your weakness requires strength. It shows strength and builds strength. And guess who hates that? The Enemy. He wants to keep us feeling alone and embarrassed, allowing condemnation to keep us from the truth. If we don't share our weaknesses, nobody knows, and if nobody knows, how can they speak truth into us? And the cycle continues of us feeling shame, alone and embarrassed, trying to figure it all out on our own. But when we confess our weaknesses to God and let safe friends in, the lie gets exposed, and it loses its power. True humility is more honorable than the greatest first-place trophy we could ever earn.

Letting others into your weakness is never fun, but it will build a deeper relationship between you and them. It doesn't matter whether that weakness is physical or something you hold close to your chest and only let a few trusted friends into. You will have a deeper and stronger relationship with those trusted friends because of it. And you will be more humble, more honored by God, and a better person.

Making Space for God's Strength in Our Weakness

Weakness isn't the curse it often appears to be. Actually, when we are weak, it allows God's strength the space to come through for us. We see this played out in the striking example of the apostle Paul. He didn't like the weakness in him that the Enemy caused, so he cried out to God. The answer God gave the steadfast apostle continues to teach and inspire us today. Paul writes,

> To keep me from becoming proud, I was given a thorn in my flesh, a messenger from Satan to torment me and keep me from becoming proud.

Three different times I begged the Lord to take it away. Each time he said, "My grace is all you need. My power works best in weakness." So now I am glad to boast about my weaknesses, so that the power of Christ can work through me. That's why I take pleasure in my weaknesses, and in the insults, hardships, persecutions, and troubles that I suffer for Christ. For when I am weak, then I am strong.

2 Corinthians 12:7–10

Paul understood that weakness is actually a good thing because it shows Christ's power. It's not a bootstrap attitude of *I can do it. Just try harder, think better, believe more, and then all will be well.* If you've been trying to face it all on your own, you don't have to. If you feel weak, it's okay because when you are weak, He is strong!

Justin, a good friend of mine, surprised me one day when he told me he was envious of me because of my weakness.

"What? You're envious of me because there are so many things I can't do?"

"Yep."

"Why?"

"Because you have to rely on God for everything. I don't have to."

There are so many things he can do on his own; he doesn't need to rely on or trust God for the same things I do. It took me a while to take it as a compliment. I don't like having to rely on God for everything. He needs to provide help or care for me every day, 365. Even when I sleep and I can't roll over in bed at night. If my wife isn't home or I'm on the road, someone must sleep close enough to hear me yell for help to roll over. But the truth is, Justin's observation is correct. There are so many areas where I need to depend on God to provide me with help, and I am blessed every single time someone steps in to answer God's call. Yet, truth be told, my need for God's interaction in my life extends way beyond my physical needs. That's true for all of us, regardless of whether we need help getting rolled over in bed or lifted into a *tap tap*.

In our self-sufficient culture, we have become independent to a fault. Only God knows how many of His blessings we miss in our fierce determination to be able to handle life on our own. Countless self-help books and motivational leaders have steered eager followers away from the one true place where our strength comes from. When we raise the white flag and admit our weaknesses to God, when we rely on Him, that's when the power of Christ helps us do more than we ever thought possible.

Letting Our Weakness Bring Blessings

I have experienced blessings in the middle of my weaknesses so many times. I have deeper relationships because of the sacrifice of others. For years my friend Jay would come to my house every day after lunch to help me stand up so I could go back to work. He's traveled with me, lifted me, and changed his own plans at the last minute so he could drive to get me when I was stranded three-and-a-half hours away in a broken-down vehicle. Jay is a classic example of the sacrifice of humility. Jay humbly serves.

It also takes humility to receive, and sometimes that is just plain difficult to do. But we must be careful not to take away someone else's blessing because of our own pride. (Have you noticed yet how much I struggle with pride? Thank you to those of you who admit you struggle with pride as well. I admire your humility.)

My Dutch background makes pride a thing to be reckoned with. I was taught to not show weakness. *Don't let others know you're struggling. You don't need help. You can figure this out on your own.* But when you are always strong, you deprive others of the blessings God has for them as they come alongside you.

When I was traveling for a speaking engagement with a friend of mine a few years ago, we missed what God was wanting to do. After the church service, we packed up and hit the road. As we were driving, my friend told me, "I had a guy come up to me after the service and offer me some cash."

"Well, what did you say?"

"Nah, we don't need that. You keep it."

I don't remember the amount or if we needed it. That's not the important part. Suddenly the Holy Spirit hit me upside the head. I'm not sure if the Holy Spirit does that to you, but it sure felt like a slap upside the head to me. It wasn't about the money, and quite frankly it wasn't about us. It was about what God was doing through that gentleman. The blessing wasn't for us. It was for a generous stranger. It was about him being obedient to what God was calling him to do. We have no idea what God was doing through him and wanted to teach him. In rejecting his kind offer, we took away his blessing. Our pride got in the way. Pride has a way of doing that.

I'm not proud to say there have been other times I've let my pride prevent what God was wanting to do for another person. I was in a store in California, buying some Disneyland shorts (don't ask me why), and I was chatting with the kid who was working there. Then God nudged me the way He sometimes does. I heard, "Pray for him."

Nope. I'm in California of all places, God. I'm not doing it. I might have even shaken my head at God in my silent conversation with Him.

I walked out of that store without following through, never knowing what would have happened if I had obeyed God's nudge. Did this kid need someone to step into his weakness with him? I'll never know. What I do know is that kid missed the blessing of an unexpected prayer, and I missed the blessing of being humbly obedient. My pride got in the way. I'd venture to say this happens to most of us. God may be wanting to speak to another person through us but we too often let our pride get in the way.

I recently heard from a friend who followed the nudge. Ron had been loading up some lumber at the local lumber yard, chatting casually with one of the hands who was helping him. They were just talking back and forth like guys do. How ya doin'? Do you like your job? Yada yada yada.

Once the lumber was all loaded, the yard hand asked my friend Ron, "Anything else?"

"Nope, I'm good." The hand walked back toward the store as my friend headed to open the door of his truck. He then felt an urgency, a voice inside of him say, "Go back and pray with him."

At first Ron tried to ignore it. He could imagine the guy snapping back at him, "I don't want you praying for me. Get outta here, you freak." Fear threatened his pride. But the nudge was so strong Ron stopped midstep. Then he told me it was like Jesus stood beside him and elbowed him, saying, "Did you hear what I said? Go back and talk to him!"

So my friend turned around. He yelled at the yard hand, "Hey! Just one more thing."

The guy stopped and looked back. "Yeah. What do you need?"

The two men walked toward each other. "It's more like, What do you need?" Ron said. "How can I pray for you?"

"Oh, thanks for asking!" At that moment, the lumber yard employee unloaded his story. He had just gotten out of prison and was on a temporary work release in the loading yard, his future uncertain. He talked a mile a minute.

My buddy took off his hat and put his arm around the ex-con's shoulder. He asked God to show this man that He is faithful, that when it all looks dismal in our eyes, God sees the truth, that we can depend on Him. Amen. A short, simple prayer. That's all.

The lumber guy teared up and hugged my friend. "Thank you, man. I needed that."

My friend asked him if he had a place to get connected and encouraged him to go to church, that God will meet him there.

"I know that," the man replied. "He's been meeting me everywhere I go."

Ron walked back to the pickup feeling ten pounds lighter. The yard hand walked back to the lumber yard whistling.

If my buddy hadn't obeyed in humility, if he'd let his weakness of not knowing what to say or the fear of rejection stand in the way, would God have sent someone else to pray with this desperate ex-con? Would that person have been part of God's blessing? Did God send someone else to pray for the kid in the Disneyland store? Only God knows. I do know that God uses the weak, the humble, and the obedient. And I want to be used by God, don't you?

God works in mysterious ways, and sometimes we think it's all about us, when in reality God is working just as much in the other person's life. A vulnerability and a yes to receiving help can be just what the other person, the one helping us in our weakness, needs. Some days I need to remind myself of that more than once.

On one occasion I was in a bind and needed help (see a theme here?). I was invited to be a part of an event but needed someone to physically help me throughout the evening. I was telling my friend Adrie about it, not even remotely thinking he would be the one to help me. Adrie is a longtime donor who runs a successful, high-profile business with thousands of employees. I mean, the guy sits at the head of a conference table and deals with top executives, the custom-tailored suit kind of guys.

"I'll do it." He volunteered.

"What?" I hesitated. Truthfully, I felt a little intimidated. Adrie has way bigger things to deal with than helping me get up from chairs, unfold my ramp so I could get into the building, or lift me in front of the crowd so I could do what I was asked to do.

But that's what this humble CEO did. Not once did I hear him complain or say, "Well, that was embarrassing." Rather than being the man on stage in charge of directing everything, which would be his usual role, Adrie was blessed to get to be a normal guy helping out a friend. We were both blessed that night. But

I almost let my pride get in the way of letting him help me. I'm glad I accepted his offer.

This journey of life is unique for each one of us. When we are vulnerable and open, God uses us, and both the receiver and giver are blessed. Our weakness is one of the most powerful ways God shows His strength.

PRAYER

Dear Lord, help me see that my weakness is actually the strength you give me through Jesus. Thank you for showing me the beauty of humility and for the times you gently remind me to humble myself. When I feel your nudge, help me swallow my pride and obey you. Don't let me get in the way of the blessing you want to give them or the blessing you have for me. Thank you, Lord, for your strength that has power in my weakness. I love that you use me in spite of my weaknesses. I love you.

In your precious name I pray, Jesus,
Amen.

TRUE FOR ME

Christ works through me (2 CORINTHIANS 12:9).

I am strong in my weakness (2 CORINTHIANS 12:9).

God gives me power when I am weak (ISAIAH 40:29).

The Holy Spirit helps me when I am weak (ROMANS 8:26).

God gives me a strong spirit (2 TIMOTHY 1:7).

Jesus understands my weakness (HEBREWS 4:15).

God helps others through my weakness (2 CORINTHIANS 13:9).

7

Just Roll with It

aughter is good for the soul. I mean, what is more infectious than an unstoppable belly laugh? I love when that happens to me, and I love hearing others about to bust a gut. My daughter Riley has a sidesplitter laugh that I especially love to hear. I always say, "I'd rather laugh than cry." Who wouldn't? But when you feel broken, unseen, unloved, and forgotten, tears seem to be more frequent than laughter. Still, it's important to laugh . . . because if we don't, we'll cry, and no one wants to cry all the time.

No one had more cause to cry all the time than poor Job in the Bible. The faithful guy had been blindsided when the Enemy destroyed everything he loved. We would cry too. And Job's friends didn't help. His friend Bildad points his finger at Job as being an "evildoer" who God had cast away. Surely Job must have done something to make God mad at him, Bildad accuses. He has the audacity to say that God would fill Job's heart with joy and restore his circumstances, if only Job stopped being such a bad guy (see Job 8:20–21). How ridiculous! Who needs friends like that?

If each of us could be transparent with one another, we'd have to admit we have all disappointed God. Plenty. I used to wonder if my diagnosis was a punishment from God. But there are evil-hearted, guilty criminals on death row who are physically healthier than I am, you know what I mean? The thought process that MD is God's punishment just doesn't make sense, yet the Enemy tries to weigh us down with these kinds of accusations: We made the wrong decision; that's why we're suffering. You were mean to your grandma; that's why you have cancer. I am not a perfect leader; that's why my ministry struggles financially at times. Do you hear how the Enemy tries to convince us we're to blame for our brokenness? Even worse, he wants us to believe we are forever trapped in our brokenness, left in the dark without hope. Ha! Now that makes me laugh. How wrong that is! At times like these when you feel smothered in shame and hopelessness, shift your focus to the truth—God loves you with a limitless love and He wants the best for you, regardless of how desperate your situation may seem at the moment.

Don't Take Life So Seriously

I find one of the most effective ways to resist the Enemy and the slump of depression is through the gift of laughter. It's so important to laugh, to declare God's truth in the face of the Enemy and his lies. When we refuse to give in to the accusations from the father of lies, he has to scram, skedaddle, hit the trail. God's Word says so: "Resist the devil, and he will flee from you" (James 4:7). I'm not suggesting you laugh at the Enemy; I suggest you allow your heart to be so filled with the joy of the Lord that holy laughter overflows and spills onto the devil's face.

One of Israel's great leaders, Nehemiah, led a broken group of people to rebuild Jerusalem's broken-down walls in spite of the odds stacked against them. As the people listened to the priest and teacher Ezra and the leaders read from the book of the law of God, the crowd wept. Commentators hold different opinions on why the people were crying. Some say the crowd wept because they hadn't heard God's Word in such a long time it stirred deep emotion within them; others claim the people felt shame for wandering away from the law and were afraid they would be punished; some say listeners cried from sheer awe (I might say outright fear, but that's just me) at the power of the law.

Whatever the cause for the weeping, Nehemiah knew that sacred day wasn't meant for sadness but for celebration. He put a stop to their downhearted, self-focused sadness. He instructed the people to celebrate, not mourn or weep. "'Don't be dejected and sad,'" Nehemiah said, "'for the joy of the LORD is your strength!'" (Nehemiah 8:10). Then he told the people to put on a festive meal with rich foods. Party time!

I love it when God calls a party, don't you? God loves His people, including you and me, and desires for us to have times of fun and laughter. God wants us to know His joy. In His infinite wisdom, He understands we can't stay in a way-too-serious, down-in-the-dumps mindset for very long before despair settles in. Sometimes we simply need to celebrate!

The Enemy doesn't want that to happen. He's the biggest party pooper ever. To be sure, he is much worse than a party pooper—the Enemy is downright nasty. He takes evil pleasure in stealing joy. I mean, evil. Intentional. Destructive. He seizes any opportunity he can to kill our spirit, much less a celebration. To keep us feeling hopelessly and forever broken, Satan flashes shame and fear of God's punishment in front of our eyes, trying to blind us from the forgiving joy God wants for us.

Nothing, however, can separate us from the love and joy of our loving Father. No shame. No guilt. No accusation can hold back God's love. So when God calls a party, let's go!

The people did as Nehemiah instructed. In addition to eating a hearty meal and sharing gifts of food with one another, they renewed their faith and changed their ways, ultimately staring shame in the face and replacing it with God's joy.

How do we find the joy of the Lord? In His presence. David relied on the promised joy of God's presence in the middle of a time of brokenness and great distress. "I know the LORD is always with me. I will not be shaken, for he is right beside me. No wonder my heart is glad, and I rejoice. My body rests in safety.... You will show me the way of life, granting me the joy of your presence and the pleasures of living with you forever" (Psalm 16:8–9, 11). For those of us with physical distress, this psalm resonates even more sweetly. My body rests in safety. I like that. Maybe even in a heavenly hammock. However, these words from David apply to all of us in so many ways. The Lord is always with us, and He will not allow us to be shaken away from His presence.

And in His presence, we find the purest joy. Of course, joy and laughter are not the same thing. There will be times of serious joy, a deep peace that doesn't necessarily make you laugh your head off. But there can be other times, many, many times, when a lighthearted joy will bubble up and out with life-filled laughter because of the presence of God's Holy Spirit in our soul.

We don't need to take life so seriously. Even though your heart or your dreams may be broken, my friend, God will show you the way of life and grant you the joy of His presence if you let Him. The weight of being broken is also lightened when we identify with one another in our brokenness, even when our brokenness is different from others. Job's friends were broken too, except they didn't realize it. Their self-righteousness prevented them from seeing the truth, from being the support Job needed. They were the wrong people to help Job. The right people will not only help you see the truth; they will help you to not take yourself so seriously. Great friends remind you that laughter is healing and that awkward moments make for great stories later.

I find myself in some pretty awkward situations. Being di-agnosed with a progressive, muscle-wasting disease makes for plenty of problematic moments that most people don't experience. Having friends to laugh with definitely makes things better. That doesn't mean life is always going to be rainbows and unicorns. Sometimes you need a bathroom bouncer. The bouncer's job is to make sure everything goes okay (no pun intended). My friend Jay is great at this role. He's one of the best bathroom bouncers. I feel bad for him because he is usually standing in the corner of the men's room waiting for me to finish up. He looks like some strange dude hanging out in the bathroom as other guys come in, but he handles it like a champ. He's got my back even when it's uncomfortable.

Jay and I entered the facilities at a concert, and things didn't smell great (it *was* the men's room). Jay helped me stand from my chair, and I started making my way to the urinal. The floor was slippery (it *was* the men's room).

"Man, it smells in here. Hurry up." Jay was ready to bolt. "I'll wait for you outside."

"No. Stay here. I'm starting to slip."

He stayed with me like the champ he is. As I finished, a stall door opened and a little kid came out with Kleenex shoved up both nostrils. Jay, without missing a beat, patted him on the head. "Hey little buddy, I used to get those all the time too." We waited until the boy left the restroom before we laughed out loud.

Jay is about eighteen years older than I am. I'm proud of him and his efforts to help in any way he can. Jay has his own battle with physical obstacles. He has survived a stroke, a brain tumor, and recently, another fight with a tumor, but it's not obvious unless you know him. His left side is affected, yet he never complains. He embraces each day with laughter and helps those he can, even in the awkward moments. Jay's attitude inspires me to keep enjoying the journey. That's why I love to travel with him.

Jay accompanied me on one of my favorite trips to North Carolina for a conference with the John Maxwell Group. One of the nightly activities at the conference included the participants getting a ride in a NASCAR car around Charlotte Motor

Speedway. As much as I wanted to take a turn, I didn't think it was going to be possible.

Then I heard, "We'll get you in the car!" *Good ol' Jay.* He was determined I wouldn't miss this opportunity and recruited the attendants to help get me in the car, not an easy feat. NASCAR doors don't open, requiring the Dukes of Hazzard entry. So one person put my legs in the car. Another person held my chest and waited to push my butt in. But it was a gal. I think she was afraid to grab my butt, so I said, "Just touch it; my wife won't mind." A little push on the tush and into the car I went, with Jay supervising to make sure no one dropped me.

We sped around the track at 160 miles per hour. Yes, I'll admit I was praying as we went around the track. When we finally stopped, I thanked God we didn't crash, and then I thanked Jay for making sure I didn't miss out on that exhilarating experience. I couldn't stop giggling, my heart still beating fast from the unbelievable adventure. Five laps around Charlotte Motor Speedway at 160 miles per hour. Now you're living! Of course, then the crew had to pull me out of the car. Not quite a Dukes jump, but we accomplished it, all of us chuckling by the time they landed me back into my chair.

My children, Jager, Riley, and Aidan, have all grown up with a disabled dad. They have been there through the processes of my body not doing what it used to do. As the only son, Jager jumps in and helps with those more intimate needs. It's totally awkward to have your son help you in and out of the shower, but it can make for good laughs as well. On one trip, I was having a little trouble standing in the shower. I yelled for Jager's help. He came running and held onto me so I wouldn't fall. In the walk-in shower, there was a seat folded up on the wall.

"Jager, unfold that seat so I can sit on it."

My not-so-brilliant plan included me having to sit on my poor son's knee while he concentrated on unfolding the seat and not dropping me at the same time.

I snickered after we returned home as I overheard Jager tell my wife, "Mom, my knee will never be the same."

For those in the disability community, these kinds of stories are everyday life. Awkward moments happen all the time. But whether a person has a disability or not, awkward moments will happen. It's called life. A beautiful, messy, we-need-each-other, may-as-well-laugh life.

It's not surprising how much life we can miss out on because of fear, pride, or the desire for self-sufficiency. That doesn't need to happen. Let's not let our brokenness rob any more joy from our lives. Don't miss out in life just because you're scared, don't want to show your weakness, or don't want to ask for help.

Don't Miss Out Because You're Scared

Fear is a paralyzer. It makes us ineffective and sends us into hiding, afraid of what might happen if our brokenness overpowers us. My friend Ken Davis asked me once, "Why are you trying so hard to fit in when you were made to stand out?" I wanted to be the star quarterback, not the guy who strutted awkwardly down the halls. I never wanted to stand out for being different. The idea terrified me. So that's my answer, Ken. I was scared.

Over the years I've gained a new perspective on fear. Point blank, unwarranted fear doesn't come from God. Self-protective fear? Yes, there are times fear is necessary, and I thank God for it. For example, if a wife is afraid of her abusive husband, that fear serves as a warning signal to take shelter. That's warranted fear. I'm talking about fear that doesn't necessarily have any weight to back it up, fear that doesn't represent danger. The kind of fear that might predict embarrassment, rejection, a lack of confidence, failure, emotionally painful stuff like that. That's the kind of fear that paralyzes us, stopping us from living a full life. But God gives us a much better gift.

"For God has not given us a spirit of fear and timidity, but of power, love, and self-discipline" (2 Timothy 1:7). Paul writes those words to his friend and mentee Timothy, reminding him to keep the faith when times get tough. We know all about tough times, don't we? When we let this truth sink into our souls, we can live to the full. Power. Love. Self-discipline. These gifts speak into our brokenness. You have the ability to face your adversity because of the Holy Spirit within you. God fills you with an endless love. His faithful presence in you will give you the strength to do what needs to be done to live in the fullness God desires for you.

The spirit of fear and timidity that taunts all of us at one time or another does not come from God. Instead, He empowers us to face the fear, to get the upper hand on it because Christ lives in us. And when you and I lean into that truth, that's when we can live a full life of power and love.

Through all my trials, I've seen God show His love for me over and over again. The truth is nobody has an easy road in this life. In one way or another, we all have had disasters and setbacks, trauma and tragedy, ups and downs. They happen to all of us. The important thing to remember is that God loves you, made you, and promises to never leave you as you go through life. "God has said, 'I will never leave you or let you be alone'" (Hebrews 13:5 NLV). He's like the proverbial big brother who always has our back. That truth helps lower the fear factor, doesn't it?

So, my friend, in the middle of our brokenness, our differences, let me encourage you. Standing out isn't something to be fearful of, but rather something to embrace. When we accept the fact that every person's life is different in one way or another, that each of us experiences brokenness, we find the freedom to be ourselves. We are each a unique creation. It doesn't matter whether you're tall or short, thin or the opposite of thin. Whether your skin is white, black, brown, or something in between. Whether you're physically abled or physically challenged. You are loved. You are valued. You matter.

We can either let the fear of standing out paralyze us from living life, or we can learn to laugh, to not take ourselves so seriously, to even treasure those awkward moments.

Don't Miss Out Because You Don't Want to Show Weakness

My heart longs for adventure, yet my physical weakness usually stands in the way. And if there is a way for me to participate in an adventure, I don't like showing my weakness. In my heart of hearts I just want to be a normal Joe doing all the regular things other guys do. But that's not my reality. God showed His goodness again by allowing me to do something that looked impossible for someone with my condition.

The opportunity to skydive came up while we were visiting Sharla's parents in Arizona one Christmas break. She really wanted to go. So, being the loving husband that I am, I said, "Let's do it." Okay, I'm not going to lie. I'm a competitive guy and everyone else in Sharla's family had already been skydiving. I didn't want to be *that guy* who was too chicken to try, regardless of my physical limitations. I didn't want to receive another "Get over it!" lecture. So yes, I said, "Let's do it." That also meant I had to ask for help and be willing to receive it, no matter how embarrassing that might be.

As the time for our dive neared, Sharla didn't know it, but my confidence was quickly fading. *What if something goes wrong? What if this is it?* Then my father-in-law added to the pressure. "Are you sure you want your kids there in case you bounce off the ground?"

Before we headed to the airfield, I called home to Jay. "Hey, if we don't make it, will you take the kids?"

The other line was quiet for a minute. "Sure, but only for six months, and then they're all going to different homes." He was kidding, I think.

We headed to the skydiving site where we signed the papers, watched the safety video (though I still couldn't see what safety there is if something goes wrong), and went outside to get suited up.

As we waited for the plane to come in, I went to the bathroom five or six times. I didn't want my nerves to make me land on the ground with wet pants. We went over how it was going to work jumping tandem with my partner. They weren't sure how my body was going to take the free-fall pressure, and since duct tape fixes just about anything, that was our plan. Duct-tape Rob to his skydiving partner.

The plane came in, and we all climbed aboard. My wife was super excited. I was fighting back tears. I hoped I didn't look like a scaredy cat.

As the airplane climbed to thirteen thousand feet, a couple of guys set me on my partner's lap and duct-taped my arms to his arms. They left my legs unconnected.

My father-in-law gave me one last piece of advice. "You'd better keep your mouth shut because you might not get it closed again with the air pressure." That was one of those times I thought, *I hear you, but it sounds like a challenge to me.* I'm not always as smart as I wish I was.

It was now our turn to jump. My jumping partner stood and kind of dragged me to the door. He gave me quick instructions. "Make sure your toes are on the edge when we go out." Well, because he dragged me, my feet were behind me. He lunged once, twice, and I kept thinking, *Wait! My feet are behind me! You told me to have them at the edge!* But it was too late.

Out the door we went. He had a helmet on; I did not. I'm still not sure what that was all about, but of course, my head hit the overhead door as we exited the airplane. Thankfully there was no damage to my hard skull as my face hit the cold air. It felt like little needles hitting my cheeks. I opened my mouth just to be rebellious (I did get it closed, for the record, no problem) and then it was time to pull the chute. One, two, three, and the chute was pulled. We were now soaring like an eagle. I could see for miles and miles up there, the air current carrying us gently as we gradually lowered to the ground.

As we were coming down to land, my partner asked, "Can you pull your legs up before we hit the ground?"

"No, we talked about this."

"Try."

Okay. Here we go. I reached down and tried to pull up my legs, but all that happened was I pulled up my jumpsuit.

The ground was coming closer and closer. *Oh no, what do I do?* I kept trying to pull my legs up, but all I did was expose my ankles. And then we hit the ground. One leg went one way and the other another. You could see our skid marks, but nothing was broken, and we were back on the ground. My partner helped me get my legs straightened out as everyone on the ground rushed over and asked me what I thought about the dive.

All of a sudden, I heard screaming with excitement. It was my wife. Sharla had just landed. She'd loved every minute of it. I was shaking a little and happy to be back on the ground. At the same time, I felt such gratitude for the adventure. I may have looked funny doing the splits on our landing, and I may or may not have had bugs in my mouth, but at that point I didn't care. I was so thankful I didn't let my fear of showcasing my weakness stop me from experiencing this incredible adventure with my wife.

What about you? Is there an adventure calling your name, but fear blocks you from trying something new? Or, like me, does the shame of weakness prevent you from embracing life in full swing, making you afraid you'll fail or damage something in the process? I'm right there with you. Together let's commit to no longer allowing fear to paralyze us and steal our victories, no matter how small. If you long to live life to the full, say yes to the invitation, climb into a seat of confidence, and buckle yourself in for the ride. Let's do this!

Don't Miss Out Because You Don't Want to Ask for Help

On this I know I'm not alone. Very few people like to ask for help, especially guys. Needing to ask for help seems to come with a weakling reputation, as though real men don't need to ask for help. Ever. Of course, we've all seen the comical results as a result of that faulty confidence. Others watch and try not to laugh while a macho man attempts to do it all on his own. Almost all families have those stories that are repeated at every reunion. We laugh at the lighthearted stories when someone didn't ask for help when they should have.

But the stories we don't revisit are the ones that didn't happen. The life that is missed because someone didn't want to ask for help—a college student didn't seek help and didn't graduate; a lonely person missed the special occasion, too depressed to reach out; an overwhelmed mom kept her kids at home rather than joining the neighborhood playgroup. We all have legitimate times of needing help, and I mean all of us. No one is exempt from needing help, more often than any of us want to admit. And how sad is that? So much of life is missed because we don't want to ask for help.

If we can accept the beauty of asking, receiving, and giving help, how much easier and full all of our lives would be. My life is an example of how asking for help and receiving it can actually be a joyful blessing. I wouldn't wish MD on anybody, but I would love for everyone to experience these kinds of help-filled interactions with other members of the body of Christ.

From the time Jager was big enough to hold part of my weight, he'd been my guy helping in the morning when Sharla left for work and then meeting me at the office to get me in the door. Those moments meant a lot to me. However, kids grow up and God calls them to their own dreams. When Jager joined the National Guard after high school, God raised up a young college student, Parker, to help me. Parker was taking classes online due to the Covid outbreak and was able to help for a year and a half. I dreaded that Parker would be leaving. Discussing this with my friend Jack, he answered me with, "Maybe it's not about why God took Parker, but rather who's next?"

Then Julie, a mom who serves on our RiseFest team, came to my office with her sixteen-year-old son, Jarrett. I shared the news that my helper would soon be leaving. "He'll help," Julie said, pointing at her son. He didn't argue, say yes, or anything. I'm pretty sure nothing came out of his mouth. He just listened to his mom and agreed. Thankfully, Jarrett wasn't afraid to step up to the challenge of traveling with a grown man with muscular dystrophy.

Jarrett's first trip with me was to a local meeting to meet another friend's cousin to see if he could help out when Jarrett went back to school, so it wasn't super intense. I just needed him to lift me in and out of the car, out of the wheelchair to use the bathroom, etc. After the meeting, we loaded up and headed home.

Jarrett finally found his voice. "Well, that was kind of like a date."

"Shut up."

But he was right. We had to see if our personalities would click because I was going to be needing a lot of his help. God brought other helpers as well, guys like Eddie. Eddie comes from Compton, California, and has had a different upbringing than mine. He's been stabbed, shot, has spent time in prison and was looking for some work. We had some work around the office and on the RiseFest grounds, so we brought him on. And when my personal helpers' schedules got changed, I asked Eddie to step into that role. God raised up Eddie in a whole new way.

I now have a team of helpers, friends who are willing to step in to help out when needed. I just need to ask. God is using this crazy story of MD in ways I hadn't planned or ever saw coming. Asking for help does not make you weak or less than. Actually it makes you stronger, as crazy as that sounds. Asking for help requires humility and vulnerability. The joy that comes from letting the right people into your life is so worth it.

Let me encourage you today to move beyond the barrier that holds you back from asking for help. Don't let fear, pride, embarrassment, or whatever obstacle you're dealing with cause you to miss out on life. When you ask for help, you might be surprised at what happens next. Who knows? Once you admit you need help and reach out, you might be giving another macho man or superwoman permission to do the same.

Laughter Is Good for the Soul

Awkward moments create laughter. Just think about your most embarrassing moment; doesn't it bring a smile to your face? When you share that story with a friend, don't you both laugh? Me too. It is so important for us to allow funny memories and current humor to live in our hearts, to let laughter flow from within. We simply can't allow ourselves to wallow in despair. That kind of darkness has a powerful pull. We know it all too well.

There are days our brokenness is all we can see, and yes, I agree, it's hard to laugh on those days. So on those days, treat yourself with tender care and sit in the presence of the Lord, allowing His light to bring hope and cheerfulness to your heart. Turn on praise music and find a spot in the sunshine if possible. And ask God to meet you in your broken spirit and cheer your heart with His light and strength. Pick up your Bible to renew your mind with the cleansing, healing, strengthening Word of God. The psalms are always a good place to find encouraging comfort. As you surrender your broken spirit to God, feel His presence fill your heart. That's the best medicine. "A cheerful heart is good medicine, but a broken spirit saps a person's strength" (Proverbs 17:22). Rather than moping in our brokenness, we can choose to recall those times that bring cheerfulness to our minds. And yes, laughter.

My daughter Aidan doesn't seem to share the same adventure bug I have, so when I would take her tubing behind the pontoon, she didn't like going fast. I've already told you I like to drive fast. That includes pontoons.

I explain to Aidan that creeping around the lake dragging a tube behind the pontoon isn't my favorite thing to do.

"I can take it for a while," I admit, "but then I just have to hit the throttle."

So we compromise.

"Okay, Dad. You can go fast, but only if you go in a straight line."

Sounds good to me. I give a little smirk, knowing I'll have to turn at some point to avoid hitting the shore or another boat.

Sure enough, I'm cruising along at a pretty good clip when I need to turn. As we veer to the left, I hear Aidan screaming, "Daddy, you're not invited to my wedding anymore!" She was only eleven or twelve years old at the time. Thinking ahead.

"And Grandpa's walking me down the aisle!"

Laughing out loud, I shout back to her, "Funny! Joke's on you. I can't walk anyway!"

We still laugh about that pontoon ride today.

So yes, laughter is good for the soul as it washes away darkness, filling the soul with comfort, lightness, relief. As we learn to adapt and laugh, we press on toward healing in our brokenness. Remember, it's not only okay to ask for help; it is right and good. God created us to live in community, hard times and all. These times give us a real-life picture of loving your neighbor as yourself, the way God has asked us to. Loving your neighbor as yourself, being a servant leader, puts us in awkward moments, but that doesn't have to ruin the journey. Quite the opposite . . . doing life together enhances the journey. If nothing else, it makes for some great stories to share.

PRAYER

Dear Jesus, thank you for giving us laughter and humor! Laughter is good medicine and fills my soul. When I take myself too seriously, remind me to find humor in the situation. Please don't let fear or my feeling of weakness keep me from enjoying life or going after things that may look difficult to accomplish. Help me to realize that my awkward moments can actually make great stories to help others find joy in their own moments. I thank you, Jesus, that I can laugh and that I have friends to laugh with me on this journey of life.

In your precious name I pray,
Amen.

TRUE FOR ME

God fills me with laughter (PSALM 126:2–3).

God gives me a time to laugh (ECCLESIASTES 3:2–4).

God makes my heart cheerful and healthy (PROVERBS 17:22).

God gives me a glad heart and a continual feast (PROVERBS 15:13–15).

God gives me strength in His joy (NEHEMIAH 8:10).

God blesses me with laughter after weeping (LUKE 6:21).

8

Jesus Is for You

'd love to tell you that when you put your faith and trust in Jesus, all the pain and disappointment that life hits you with go away, but that isn't the way it works. Even as I write this, I've been wrestling with feeling unloved, unseen, and forgotten. Again. And I find myself asking that nagging question: *Why, God?* Again.

Well, the Bible answers that question right up front in Genesis. When Adam and Eve made the choice to listen to the devil and eat the fruit, sin entered the world. That changed everything. What was once perfect became flawed and broken. Then God showed His love for humanity by sending His only Son, Jesus, to make a way for us to be restored. And yes, there is hope for each one of us through His sacrifice on the cross. That is true. But there is still heartache and brokenness in this world. Big time. We find ourselves living in the tension of knowing there is hope and a better tomorrow on the horizon while living in the here and now that is burdened by brokenness and grief.

Since I broke my foot, I've had even more limited accessibility. I can no longer walk, even with my wife's assistance. Before I broke my foot, she could lift me out of bed or out of a chair, and then I could move around the room by myself. I could finish getting ready standing up on my own. Now she needs to lift me out of bed into the wheelchair, out of the wheelchair onto the shower chair, out of the shower back into the wheelchair, onto the toilet to get dressed, then back into the wheelchair. What used to be one to two lifts has become five to six lifts. I know the toll it's taking on her back. And at that unpleasant thought, the reality of the disease punches me in the face. Again.

I'm going to make a confession. For many years I've battled a recurring bad attitude about God. The way I have seen it is this: my body's progression with the disease equals my lack of seeing God as good. It feels like a good God would take away the pain, the adversity, the obstacles of being me. A good God wouldn't let one of His loved ones be condemned as *that guy*, less than, or worthless. Yet here I am watching my body do exactly what I hoped it would never do—get worse.

And then I remember all of the times God has met my needs, all the times I have experienced His love, all the times He has lifted me out of the dumps, and I feel His attention, presence, and reassuring love once again.

Take an Inventory of God's Faithfulness

Life seems to happen in waves. Like when you go into your local coffee shop to find yourself the lucky first person in line, only to look back a moment later to see a bunch of people waiting behind you. "Glad we got here when we did," right? Life itself ebbs and flows in almost every aspect. Peaceful seasons can last for a few days or weeks or even years, then turn on a dime when things get hard again.

When life becomes difficult, and it will, the love of Jesus can be hard to feel. We don't always feel His warm hug when we've been hit by a cold slap in the face—the slap of disappointment, tragic news, conflict in a close relationship, or life's problems in general. It is natural to feel abandoned when our feelings overshadow the truth. Taking an inventory of God's faithfulness in the good times will give you a lifeline when you need it. When we pause to recount all the times God has been faithful, it helps us in those hard times to expect Him to come through again.

For a long time, somewhere deep within me, I believed that you could only feel the love of God if you could check off everything on His list—basically by living right and not sinning. But that's simply not possible. If it were, Jesus would've never needed to go to the cross. If we could straighten up and fly right on our own, we wouldn't need a Savior. How did we ever end up with this lie of an equation that our actions determine whether God loves us? The Bible tells us the opposite. Paul writes,

> But God showed his great love for us by sending Christ to die for us while we were still sinners. And since we have been made right in God's sight by the blood of Christ, he will certainly save us from God's condemnation. For since our friendship with God was restored by the death of his Son while we were still his enemies, we will certainly be saved through the life of his Son.
>
> Romans 5:8–10

Jesus died for us while we were still sinners and enemies, not living right, that's for sure.

That verse is the complete opposite of what our minds so often tell us: If life is hard again, then we're being punished for some reason. That's why we can't feel His love. More than once I've let myself get sucked into the idea that my screw-up this time must have been the last straw for God, as if His patience has some breaking point. Although God has been faithful many times before, it is still possible for my mind to take me to, "What if He doesn't come through this time because I was being so stupid?" I hope I'm not the only one who's ever thought that.

I had a friend tell me once, "It hurts my heart that you talk to yourself the way you do. You would never talk to someone else struggling that way. You would share with them how much God loves them and how nothing can separate them from His love." And she was right. I do believe God would never leave *you* nor forsake *you*! It's me I'm not so sure about.

This is a common point of view for many of us, I've come to realize. We mistakenly think God will do for others what He's not willing to do for us. We struggle to believe He loves us as much as He loves the fella who does life with God better than we do. The Enemy can really work on us when we're in this mistaken place, when we think we must be doing something wrong, or not doing something good enough. We start to doubt and question things we already know the answer to.

And we find ourselves on the merry-go-round of a works relationship with Almighty God, spinning in circles, missing the mercy of God by trying, not trusting. Do you ever find yourself there? It's time for us to get off that senseless ride. Let's put on the brakes and stop on the line of truth. There is nothing we need to do, nothing we *can* do, to earn God's love. We have been made right through the humble sacrifice of Jesus. That needs to be the number one item on our inventory list: Jesus died for you. And the second item: Jesus is for you. Always. That means He wants what's best for you, and no way will He ever leave you hanging out to dry.

When the hard times come, what will we remember? We can take a lesson from the Israelites after God parted the Jordan River for them to carry the ark of the covenant across (see Joshua 3). This was after He'd already swallowed up Pharoah's army in the Red Sea (see Exodus 14). Wandering through the wilderness for decades, eating the same food and seemingly getting nowhere, the dusty followers had plenty of hard times to knock them off course and turn away from God, even after all He had already done to set them free. That's why God told Joshua to instruct the people to pick up stones from the river and stack them into a monument as a reminder of what He had done. These "stones of remembrance" represented the hardships of their long trip as well as the Lord's deliverance, a tangible pile to help them remember God's goodness for generations.

> Then Joshua said to the Israelites, "In the future your children will ask, 'What do these stones mean?' Then you can tell them, 'This is where the Israelites crossed the Jordan on dry ground.' For the LORD your God dried up the river right before your eyes, and he kept it dry until you were all across, just as he did at the Red Sea when he dried it up until we had all crossed over. He did this so all the nations of the earth might know that the LORD's hand is powerful, and so you might fear the LORD your God forever."
>
> Joshua 4:21–24

This is such a practical way to remind ourselves of God's faithfulness so we don't forget in the thick of the hard times.

What would your stones of remembrance look like? I am reminded of mine often as I take inventory. Even my wife will remind me. "Rob, remember when God was faithful when I was on maternity leave, and we only had your income from RISE, and that wasn't even coming in every month, yet we made it through?" Or a good friend will say, "Remember when God parted the storms and allowed RiseFest to go on? The bad weather hit two miles away, but the grounds for the festival were dry." Or the time He provided a new personal assistant even though it looked like the road was at a dead end, and the time He prompted a donor to give a generous gift just when we needed it. And remember the time when . . . ? On and on the list goes. I need to pick up more stones the next time I'm at the river. How about you?

Jesus Helps Us Overcome Obstacles

It is natural for our faith to be shaken at first when we run into obstacles. When the Israelites' backs were pinned to the sea, they could never have imagined how God would part it for them so they could escape Pharoah's army just in the nick of time. Of course they were afraid. The same is only natural for us. When the CT scan reveals a mysterious mass, only someone in denial wouldn't feel a hint of terror. We all face obstacles in our lives, blockades between us and the fullness of life Jesus wants for us.

Sometimes obstacles are simple by-products of life, as trivial as a traffic jam or a misplaced password. And sometimes obstacles are strategically set up by the Enemy. He uses fear, sickness, temptation, anything he can to destroy us. Here's the good news! Jesus offers the way past Satan's obstacles by making Himself the very gate for us to pass through. "I am the gate; whoever enters through me will be saved. They will come in and go out, and find pasture. The thief comes only to steal and kill and destroy; I have come that they may have life, and have it to the full" (John 10:9–10 NIV). Obstacles become opportunities for Jesus to show His faithfulness, His goodness, so we can have life to the full. Push on through, friend. A full life is waiting for you!

As I look back, I can see where God has pushed me to see the greater work He was doing. One of those moments was back in 2001 when I received a call from the national Muscular Dystrophy Association headquarters. They'd seen a clip of Sharla and me from the previous year's telethon filmed at our local station in Sioux City, Iowa, and they wanted to have us as guests on the upcoming annual MDA Labor Day Telethon hosted by Jerry Lewis in Los Angeles. I thought they were kidding. *Obstacle #1.* The caller assured me the invitation was legit.

In the middle of August, Sharla and I flew to LA for a practice run at the emcee's briefing. When we arrived, we met several other families from around the country with stories similar to mine. As we waited backstage, there was a great deal of commotion behind the black curtain. I was so nervous. *Obstacle #2.* A single mother and her daughter with muscular dystrophy were also waiting backstage. The girl's mother asked me if I wanted to pray. Yes, please!

We bowed our heads. I imagined the other people staring at us, whispering, "What are those two screwballs doing? Are they actually praying backstage on a Hollywood set?" *Obstacle #3. Whatever.*

The time came for me to go onstage. I was told to walk to the big X on the stage, stop there, and tell my story. *Walk on stage in front of an audience. Obstacle #4.* Around 250 to 300 emcees from around the country attended the briefing; they would then air the telethon on their local networks over Labor Day weekend. Sharla and I went out on stage and practiced telling our story. If I recall correctly, we received a standing ovation from the emcees.

Two weeks later, we flew back to LA for the two-day live show at CBS Studios. We would be aired in front of nearly sixty million viewers *(um, Obstacle #5)* to share our broken story of fighting this debilitating muscle disease. On the first day, Cynthia Garrett interviewed us, and as I walked off stage, I heard Jerry Lewis saying something kind about me. I wish I could've heard it directly, but I had to get to the men's room ASAP. My nerves were getting to me. *Obstacle #6.*

The next day we had to do it all over again. I woke up early in the hotel room and heard God's voice. I didn't like what He was saying, so I argued with Him.

"No, God, do not make me say what I think I'm supposed to say. I don't want to say that. Please."

Then our phone rang. It was Shelly, my sister-in-law who tells it like it is. She needed to talk to her sister, my wife.

"Sharla! I saw you on TV yesterday. Who did your makeup? It looked terrible. Don't let them do it again." *Obstacles #7, 8, 9, and 10.*

Shelly! I'm already nervous. Now you've got my wife wound up. Are you kidding me?

Our second interview was supposed to be with Jann Carl from *Entertainment Tonight.* As we stood at the ready, I prayed again. It was more like begging than praying. "God, please don't make me say what you want me to say. The founder of MDA is Jewish, for crying out loud. I don't want to get booed off this stage." *Fear, pride, more obstacles.*

Despite all the obstacles, Jesus had my back as we walked out to the X. Jann Carl came up to me quietly, holding cue cards with questions for us. But to my surprise, she said, "Rob, I've never heard this before in all the years I've done this, but I've been told to not ask you any of these questions today. Say whatever you need to say."

God! What did you just do here?

"Thirty seconds to countdown." The stage manager glanced in my direction.

I'm going live in thirty seconds!

"Rob, the floor is yours." Jann gave me a reassuring smile.

The red light went on. The camera started. And these words came out of my mouth:

"I want to tell you today where my hope comes from, and it comes from the Lord above."

The entire audience broke into applause. It threw me off because I had everything timed that I was going to say. The reception was unbelievable. I don't have a clue what came out of my mouth after that. I don't remember what I said. I just know God woke me up at four o'clock in the morning to tell me I was supposed to share where my hope comes from. I wasn't even comfortable enough to say "Jesus." I said "Lord." And still, Jesus gave me the courage to say what I did, knowing He would ultimately get the glory. Jesus was there for me even though I was too chicken to call Him by name.

That evening we dined as guests with the president and vice president of MDA. A month after 9/11, they asked me and Sharla to serve as MDA spokespersons, a role we filled for the next decade, traveling and speaking to help raise awareness of muscular dystrophy.

I almost let obstacles like worrying about embarrassing myself get in the way of this life-changing opportunity. Jesus wouldn't let me. He was the gate for me to go through, and He gave me the courage to do what He was calling me to do.

So many obstacles in our lives become opportunities for God to show His goodness to us. Do they often turn out differently than the way we pictured them? Usually. Yes. But that's the way God does it. He explains in Isaiah 55:8, "'My thoughts are nothing like your thoughts,' says the Lord. 'And my ways are far beyond anything you could imagine.'" Beyond anything we can imagine!

Beyond what I could have imagined, in His goodness, God brought back into my life a love of mine I thought I had lost forever. Sharla comes from a farming family. Sharla's brother, Shane (my other brother-in-law), and her dad frequently loaded me in the combine, tractor, or truck, and I'd spend hours out in the field with them. For nearly seventeen years or so, I was able to run equipment and just enjoy being out on the farm. What I thought was lost at nine years old, God brought back. *I see how you did that, God. Thanks.*

You Are Not Unloved, Unseen, or Forgotten

About eight months after my young friend Tripp died, his parents could see I was still grappling with his death. I was also battling with God about some other things, personal and painful. I felt God had turned His back on me. My disease continued to progress, and my regular care team seemed to be on a constant pattern of rotating in and out, which was hard for me. On top of it all, our ministry was suffering growth pains, dragging it into a scary financial crunch. I had a hard time getting past the old lie that God takes away from me everything I love. *God, you're not taking all this from me, are you?* He had taken Tripp, why not RISE? Circumstances clouded my spiritual eyesight, and I started to feel unloved, unnoticed, and forgotten again.

Tripp died in April. That December we offered a Christmas program for those who find the holidays hard. It was advertised as something like "Come Celebrate Christmas with Other Hurting People." We asked Chad and Maria to participate in the Christmas program, to share about Tripp, their loss, and grieving. As I met with these two beautiful people in the green room before the event, they asked me if I'd watched *The Chosen*. There was a scene they thought I should see.

Now, we can debate whether *The Chosen* series is biblical, and I understand it's only a TV show, and that it's not really Jesus. He's an actor. But when my dear friends had me watch Season 3, Episode 2, I saw Jesus' face for the first time in my life. The real Jesus. If you've watched the series, I bet you have already guessed which scene I'm talking about.

On the show, one of Jesus' disciples, Little James, has an obvious physical handicap. He stands by, in pain, watching Jesus heal one broken person after another. He sees the lame man walk, the blind man see, the dead child raised back to life. And yet Little James continues following Jesus from town to town, limping the entire way, lopsided and leaning on his wooden crutch. It's enough to make a grown man cry. I did. I do. I identify with Little James. Maybe you do too. If you've been carrying the weight of your brokenness, whatever it is, for a long time, years, even decades, and it doesn't seem like the healing of your situation is on Jesus' agenda, I want to encourage you to seek Jesus for a different kind of touch. One that brings healing to your soul.

In that episode of *The Chosen*, Little James's controversial, not-exactly-biblical encounter with Jesus touched me deeply. Little James says to Jesus something like: "You don't heal me, but you still want me to go out with the others and preach your name." I'd be tempted to add, *What a crock*. And then . . . when Little James finally gets the nerve to ask Jesus why he hasn't been healed, Jesus' answer impacts my heart in a way that brings so much hope and perspective on how Jesus sees me in my brokenness, that He really does care.

Jesus tells Little James, "In the Father's will, I could heal you right now, and you'd have a good story to tell. . . . But there are already dozens who can tell that story, and there will be hundreds more, even thousands." The disciple listens as Jesus continues. "When you discover yourself finding true strength because of your weakness, and when you do great things in my name in spite of this, the impact will last for generations. Do you understand?"

"Yes," James says through his tears.

My eyes welled up with tears too, and my heart got it right along with Little James. *Yes, I understand too, Jesus. I'm right there with my little buddy James. In spite of this crippling disease, I want to love you, follow you, and point others to you, Jesus, because of how much you love me.*

For the first time in my life, I saw Jesus' face. He was telling me He understands my brokenness and that it doesn't go unnoticed, that there is purpose in the pain. Before, I'd never seen the humanness in Jesus, His compassion, His understanding. As I watched the fictionalized scene between Jesus and His much-loved, broken disciple, I felt seen and loved. It changed something in my spirit. For the first time I could see that Jesus understands how hard the fight is to love Him without physical healing.

As I shared this with my friend Ben Fuller, he led me to a Scripture that emphasizes the reward that comes when we love and trust Jesus, even when we can't see things happening the way we think they should. We can't see it all, but Jesus does, and His plan for us extends beyond our brokenness. "You love him even though you have never seen him. Though you do not see him now, you trust him; and you rejoice with a glorious, inexpressible joy. The reward for trusting him will be the salvation of your souls" (1 Peter 1:8–9).

No matter how discouraged you might feel right now, you can take comfort in knowing you are loved, seen, remembered. Jesus is for you. He loves you with an unshakable love. He tells us through the prophet Isaiah, "'Though the mountains be shaken and the hills be removed, yet my unfailing love for you will not be shaken nor my covenant of peace be removed,' says the LORD, who has compassion on you" (Isaiah 54:10 NIV). And when you feel like no one sees you, much less God, remember this: "The eyes of the LORD are on those who fear him, on those whose hope is in his unfailing love" (Psalm 33:18 NIV). In those darkest times when you're convinced you've been forgotten, God has you in His hands. Literally. It's His promise to each one of His people. That includes you and me. "I will not forget you! See, I have engraved you on the palms of my hands" (Isaiah 49:15–16 NIV). Life has its moments of deep despair when all hope looks lost, but that's not the whole story.

Jesus Will Make Things New

As followers of Jesus, we have a beautiful ending of the story waiting for us. Many of us will see our brokenness healed as we allow Him to work in our lives. We'll see relationships repaired, dreams renewed, second chances shining brighter than the first time around. Jesus wants to redeem lives. He doesn't want us trudging through life like defeated soldiers heading home from a losing battle. Remember He wants us to have abundant life here on earth.

Yet, we still live in a broken world. That means some things won't be restored until the glorious day Jesus returns. When that happens, all broken hearts will be healed. "He will wipe every tear from their eyes, and there will be no more death or sorrow or crying or pain. All these things are gone forever" (Revelation 21:4). Brokenness will be gone forever.

And wrapped around this is how He will make our broken bodies new when He returns. Oh, praise the Lord! For obvious reasons, I can't wait for that day!

"But we are citizens of heaven, where the Lord Jesus Christ lives. And we are eagerly waiting for him to return as our Savior. He will take our weak mortal bodies and change them into glorious bodies like his own, using the same power with which he will bring everything under his control" (Philippians 3:20–21).

This verse is both comforting and challenging for me. I love that the risen Jesus is coming back, and that He's going to give us new bodies. The part that gets challenging for me is the waiting. Like Little James's character has to endure his body's brokenness for the foreseeable future, it appears I do too. I still believe God could choose to heal me at any time, but until that happens, whether on this earth or as a citizen setting up house in heaven, I will choose to place my trust in Jesus. Will you join me? Because you know what, my friend? Even when it may feel we are dragging ourselves through our brokenness all alone, He is always with us.

There's a well-known poem that I think of often. Apparently a few people have claimed to have written it, which I find confusing, and I think all of them are women. So I'm going to paraphrase the story for you and tell it from my perspective. The poem tells the story of an individual looking back on his life and seeing two sets of footprints in the sand, one belonging to him and the other to the Lord as they walked through life together. Then he notices places that have only one set of footprints. It turns out those places were the darkest, hardest times of this guy's life. So he asks Jesus why He ditched him when he needed Him most. Jesus lovingly tells the guy, "Hey man, it was during those difficult times that I carried you. Those are my footprints, buddy, not yours."

I've been physically carried by family and friends for years now, so I can picture Jesus carrying me in a very realistic way. You might not have the experience of being carried up a mountain or onto a Haitian *tap tap*, but I feel certain you can still put yourself in the place of the man in the poem. For all of us who have ever cried out, "Jesus, where are you?" we can remind ourselves He is always there for us, and He wants to ease our load.

He offers us rest when we're tired, worn out, and exhausted with nothing left in the tank. He whispers, "Come to me, all of you who are weary and carry heavy burdens, and I will give you rest. Take my yoke upon you. Let me teach you, because I am humble and gentle at heart, and you will find rest for your souls" (Matthew 11:28–29).

In the hard times, let yourself climb up onto His back and let Him carry you for a while. Jesus is here for you.

PRAYER

Jesus, life is hard again, and I'm struggling to feel your love or sense your presence. Please help me to know you are near and the words that you will never leave me nor forsake me are true. Remind me that you have it all under control, that one day you will make it all new. Please give me the strength and courage to continue to trust each and every day.

In your precious name, Jesus,
Amen.

TRUE FOR ME

God will make a new way for me (ISAIAH 43:18-19).

God gives me new mercies every morning (LAMENTATIONS 3:22-24).

God will live with me in a new holy city (REVELATION 21:1-3).

Jesus is with me always (MATTHEW 28:20).

God has rescued me (COLOSSIANS 1:13-14).

God is for me (ROMANS 8:31; PSALM 46:7).

Jesus is the same yesterday, today, and forever (HEBREWS 13:8).

God is my helper who gives me life (PSALM 54:4).

God is my hope (PSALM 62:5).

God gives me peace in every situation (2 THESSALONIANS 3:16).

9

God Still Chooses You

am so very grateful for my wife. I still can't believe this beautiful girl jumped into my story, knowing the future with a muscle-wasting disease loomed in front of us. Sharla demonstrates the love of Jesus every day; I've been blessed to be the recipient of her unconditional love for years. And she's shown others the same compassionate love, many times complete strangers. Still, I've worried that this Jesus-loving woman of my dreams would reach her tipping point, that I would one day hear, "Enough is enough. I can't take it anymore." But this strong woman continues to take it with grace and humor.

A few years ago, Sharla and I were having dinner at a favorite restaurant one evening and I needed to use the bathroom. So, like we'd done a hundred times before, she accompanied me to the door of the men's room. She opened the door, and I wheeled in. This was back when I could still manage the rest of the process by myself. As I was climbing out of my wheelchair a guy came in behind me and offered help, to which I responded, "No buddy, I'm good, but thanks."

Since the guy didn't need to climb back into a wheelchair or take his time, he beat me out of the bathroom. No big deal, it happens all the time. I didn't think anything of it until we got back to our table. Sharla had a grin on her face as she sat down opposite me.

"What?" I wondered what she knew that I didn't.

Then she told me what had happened while I was in the restroom.

When the other guy came out, he asked Sharla, "Is that your husband in there?"

"That guy? No."

His eyes opened wide in surprise.

"Just kidding. Yes, that's my husband." She smiled at the man.

He chuckled at her teasing, then became serious. "I'm a pharmacist and I wondered what happened to put him in that chair. What was the accident?"

"Accident? There wasn't an accident. He has muscular dystrophy."

The stranger raised his eyebrows. "So you knew?"

"Yes, I knew."

"And you married him anyway?"

"Yes, I did."

The stranger gave her a tender look and shook his head slowly. "Now that's love." He turned and walked away, leaving Sharla to wait for me.

Yes, sir, that is the most sincere love. The sacrificial kind of love that chooses to keep loving, with no strings attached.

This selfless, confident, servant-hearted woman chose me even though she knew my body was broken. She knew it would be hard and what the long-term effects were going to be. Over the years she's learned there's much more broken in me than just my body. She still chooses to love me. I have been able to rise above adversity time and time again because I have experienced the sincerest love. Yes, from Sharla. But also from God.

God Chooses You in Your Brokenness

Broken body. Broken mind. Broken heart and soul. Just plain broken. That's where so many of us find ourselves, for so many different reasons. And if we continue to focus on being broken, it begins to wear on us, dishing out a lie to keep us stuck in our hopelessness. Brokenness wants to tell you that God is done with you.

If you've ever thought your brokenness will eventually cost you your relationship with Almighty God, you're not alone, and there's a reason. I'm not talking about only outward physical brokenness, but the inner, deep, dark places you'd prefer to not talk about. So many of us suffer the nagging thoughts of being beyond repair, beyond usefulness. Not good enough, never can be, and there's nothing we can do about it. And here's the reason we start to feel alienated from God in our brokenness: the Enemy makes his playground in the middle of thoughts like that. He wants to get us to believe that if we sin or doubt or cry one more time, especially in the areas where we already beat ourselves up the most, then God is done with us. We'll be officially un-chosen. Tossed aside and forgotten. So, we strive to get our brokenness under control or try to bury our brokenness further down and act like everything is all better, because then maybe we'll be worthy of being chosen. Not true!

As if our being chosen by God has anything to do with us. We didn't even choose Him, in all actuality. Jesus chose us as a part of the bigger plan. "You didn't choose me. I chose you. I appointed you to go and produce lasting fruit, so that the Father will give you whatever you ask for, using my name" (John 15:16). Notice Jesus doesn't say here "I chose you because you rise above the rest; you're the cream of the crop, big man on campus. How could I ever build my kingdom without you, my leading player?" Not at all. Jesus seems to specialize in choosing the broken and accomplishing His purpose through us.

None of us is worthy to be chosen by God. That's why Jesus stepped into the epicenter of the battle for me and you. It's this thing called grace that says God chooses us while we're still broken. How it must grieve Him to watch us resist His grace while we continue to unsuccessfully cope with our brokenness. How many of us have driven ourselves crazy wondering, *How can God love me, and why would He choose me, considering the temptations I fall into?* There are so many: greed, envy, lust, pride, being judgmental, hate, to name a few, and these don't always show up in a way that others can see. Most of them we can hide behind closed doors, especially closed doors of the heart. The more we resist God's grace, the more we worry about how long it will be until God gives up on us altogether. And there we sit, smack dab on the swing in the center of Satan's playground.

My good friend the apostle Paul (okay, I know we never met, but I think we would be pals), leads the way in showing us how to grasp all of this. He writes to Timothy, "This is a trustworthy saying, and everyone should accept it: 'Christ Jesus came into the world to save sinners'—and I am the worst of them all. But God had mercy on me so that Christ Jesus could use me as a prime example of his great patience with even the worst sinners. Then others will realize that they, too, can believe in him and receive eternal life" (1 Timothy 1:15–16). *Thanks for taking the rap, Paul. You know how to make a guy feel better.*

Truth is, we are all sinners. And yet, not one of us is beyond the scope of God's limitless love and patience. God has mercy for each of us in our brokenness. And He doesn't stop there! He adds grace that radiates His love for us. Dear reader, God will never give up on you. He will never stop choosing you as one of His own, because of His faithful character, His love, and His longing to be with you.

God Chooses You Because of His Faithful Character

God is faithful. What God says, He'll do, He does. The earth flooded once and never will again. God made a covenant with Noah, promising that "never again will a flood destroy the earth" (Genesis 9:11). God even provided a sign from the very reflections of nature—a rainbow—so that every time we see it in the sky, even thousands of years later, we'll be reminded of His promise from long ago. That's what the rainbow's for. It has always been about God's visual promise to us, a promise that represents His commitment and love.

God also brought the Israelites to the promised land, which He said He'd do. He raised up godly kings to lead His people well, destroyed armies with three hundred mighty men (see Judges 7), protected his faithful followers by shutting the mouths of lions for Daniel (see Daniel 6) and keeping the flames from burning up three obedient young men who refused to bow before man (see Daniel 3). He sent a fish so Jonah could finish his mission, and ultimately provided a Savior from the line of David to provide hope for the world. God did what He said He'd do.

And His faithfulness continues for us today. In His holy nature, He keeps His arms open to us, ready and waiting for us to come to Him with our brokenness, baggage, blunders and all. He promises to forgive and to help us get a better handle on life. "But if we confess our sins to him, he is faithful and just to forgive us our sins and to cleanse us from all wickedness" (1 John 1:9). So, God doesn't choose us because we're such stellar human beings; He chooses us because He is faithful to His people.

God Chooses You Because of His Love

God's love is unmatched. A holy God demonstrates His love by sending His one and only Son to die for a world that lives in rebellion to His holiness. I know, because I've been one of the rebels shaking my fist at God and storming off in the opposite direction. He loves us no matter what, whether we love Him back or not.

God doesn't force you to love Him. That's probably the greatest expression of love He offers—allowing you to choose. You can reject Him, and even if you decide to do that, He still loves you! The Bible calls that *agape* love: a fatherly, in-depth love of God for the human beings He created. This is the kind of love that isn't based on you loving God in return. A sacrificial love so great that He sent His Son to live among us for around thirty-three years to teach us, heal us, love us, and eventually forgive us through the greatest expression of love ever, by dying a horrific death on a cross—knowing not all would choose to love Him. He'll love you all the way to hell if you so choose. But oh, what a tragedy that would be.

God chooses you because of who He is. God is the very essence of love (see 1 John 4:8). It might be tempting to dismiss this as kind of a generic love. *Oh, sure, and He's got the whole world in His hands. I'm just one of billions of other screwballs on the planet who God loves.* That's not how God sees it. He loves each of us up close and personal. "Even before he made the world, God loved us and chose us in Christ to be holy and without fault in his eyes" (Ephesians 1:4). He knows each of us intimately, from before the time we were baby cells multiplying in our mother's wombs to the time our thinning hair starts falling out, and God still keeps a head count (pun fully intended there) (see Jeremiah 1:5; Matthew 10:30). God loves you, and there's nothing you can do to cause Him to love you any more or less.

God loves us beyond what our limited human minds can comprehend, and in His love He chooses us, regardless of where we are on our messy journey of brokenness and healing. He is always waiting for us to come to Him.

This love is on full display when Jesus is hanging on the cross between two thieves. One of the criminals starts giving Jesus grief:

"So you're the Messiah, are you? Prove it by saving yourself—and us, too, while you're at it!" (Luke 23:39) Notice he isn't really asking Jesus to save him; he's making fun of Jesus because he doesn't believe He can. The other thief, even as he is dying, is humble and sticks up for Jesus. "The other criminal protested, 'Don't you fear God even when you have been sentenced to die? We deserve to die for our crimes, but this man hasn't done anything wrong.' Then he said, 'Jesus, remember me when you come into your Kingdom.' And Jesus replied, 'I assure you, today you will be with me in paradise'" (Luke 23:40–43).

The humble thief didn't do anything except admit he was a sinner and ask Jesus to remember him. Jesus's love did the rest. The thief couldn't make things right on his own. Just like me and you. There's nothing we can do to earn His love. He already loves us. All we need to do is receive it.

God Chooses You Because of His Desire to Be with You

When the thief asked Jesus to remember him when He went into His kingdom, it's likely the dying criminal didn't really know what that all meant. He hadn't been a disciple of Jesus, listening and learning all about God's kingdom and His upcoming plans for resurrection. I believe the broken man simply sensed the innocence and love of Jesus, and that's what drew him to the bloody Savior next to him. And what did Jesus do? He assured the agonized criminal that they would be together in paradise that day! Not an elusive someday. This represents to me God's sincere, intense desire to be with us. No "let's get together sometime" that may never happen. Today.

That may be difficult for many of us to fully understand. I know it has seemed incomprehensible to me at times. In our Christian circles, it seems many of us have spent way too much time focusing on the fear and wrath or judgment of God, trying to please Him, to the point we've missed His grace and mercy and desire to be with us. Stop and think about this overwhelming thought for a sec. God longs to be with us now and forever! *Boom! Mind blown.*

God desired so much to be with His people that He sent His Holy Spirit to live in us. Not just with us, but inside us. Seems like one outrageous mismatch to me. But God's desire is recorded in His Word for all of us to see. "As God said: 'I will live in them and walk among them. I will be their God, and they will be my people'" (2 Corinthians 6:16). When Jesus ascended to heaven, God returned in the form of the Holy Spirit to live within each of His faithful followers, so we can be with Him and He can be with us, always.

Knowing that God desires to spend time with me makes me want to know and love Him more. You too? I encourage each of us to spend time in His Word, asking Him to reveal Himself, sharing our innermost thoughts with Him and listening for His voice, so we can comprehend how wide, how long, how high, and how deep His love is (see Ephesians 3:18).

God Chooses Unlikely Heroes

I see the criminal hanging beside Jesus as a hero, an unlikely one at that. He had the nerve to openly defend a man he believed innocent, as well as the humility to ask to be included in His kingdom, all while hanging in shame in front of a crowd of gawking onlookers. That took a lot of courage.

We read throughout the Bible how God chooses unlikely heroes. Let's look at a few.

Noah

Let's start with Noah. Most often we picture him as a great hero who obeyed God to complete a beyond impossible feat, but there are certain aspects about Noah we don't talk about that much. I don't claim to fully understand why people at that time in history lived so long. Some say it's because Adam and Eve were created to live forever and it took a while for the brokenness of the world to shorten the human life span. I guess only God knows, but still . . . who at five hundred years old starts having kids? That's when Noah did. At over five centuries old, he fathered his three sons, Shem, Ham, and Japheth. Now, that's old. Really old. And building the ark didn't happen overnight. Scholars predict it took somewhere in the time frame of fifty to one hundred years to build it. Then old Noah was on the huge boat for over a year with his family and the animals (see Genesis 5–8).

We see children's books and playsets full of animals and a happy Noah, implying the assumption they lived happily ever after once they disembarked. But after the flood, Noah planted a vineyard and produced wine. One day he got drunk and naked, bringing shame and curses to the family, and lived for another 350 years after the great flood while his descendants repopulated the earth (see Genesis 9). Now I'm not going to call Noah an old drunk, but I do think it's safe to say he was an unlikely hero.

Abraham

The father of many nations, Abraham is also commonly referred to as the father of faith. When God asked Abraham to sacrifice his son, Isaac, the obedient father positioned his son on the altar, fully willing to trust God to fulfill His promise that Abraham's descendants would one day be as numerous as the stars of the sky. I guess that meant Abraham believed God could fulfill His promise with or without Isaac. Another son, perhaps? As impossible as that seemed, Abraham had already experienced the impossible miracle of Isaac's birth despite Abraham and Sarah's old age (see Genesis 21). It wouldn't be impossible for God to make that happen again. Or did Abraham somehow believe deep down that God wouldn't make him follow through with the gruesome task of driving a knife through his own son's heart? We don't know exactly what Abraham was thinking as he prepared his only, miraculous son for sacrifice. What we do know is that "'Abraham believed God, and God counted him as righteous because of his faith'" (Galatians 3:6). The apostle Paul goes on to tell us "The real children of Abraham, then, are those who put their faith in God" (Galatians 3:7). So there you have it. For generations since he walked this earth, Abraham has been known as the father of faith. And God blessed Abraham's faith by providing a ram to sacrifice instead of Isaac (see Genesis 22).

But I've gotta ask: Where was Abraham's faith earlier when God promised him Isaac in the first place? He got tired of waiting and started to think it wasn't going to happen. When he and his wife got to be around one hundred years old, he listened to his wife's counsel instead of God's and slept with her maidservant Hagar, resulting in a son, Ishmael (see Genesis 16).

And I've often wondered about Abraham's faith the two times he passed off his beautiful wife, Sarah, as his sister. They had traveled to godless places—first to Egypt, then to Philistine territory—and Abraham feared that each land's ruler would kill him to take Sarah as his wife (see Genesis 12:10–20 and 20:1–18). I'm not judging. Abraham was a man of great faith, yes, but it seems he still dealt with impatience, fear, and doubt. Just like the rest of us.

Moses

Moses was a Hebrew raised as an Egyptian. As an infant, Moses was spared by Pharaoh's daughter when she found him in a basket floating down the Nile River. His name means, "drawn forth, taken out of the water" (see Exodus 2:1–10). One day he saw an

Egyptian beating a Hebrew slave. In his anger, Moses killed the abusive Egyptian. After being noticed for his crime, he fled to Midian where God revealed Himself to Moses in a burning bush and called him to lead His people out of slavery. Moses reminded the Almighty of his stutter, which didn't make for diplomatic conversations with higher-ups like Pharoah (see Exodus 2:11–15; Exodus 3:1–4:17). Finally giving in and following through on what God asked of him, Moses didn't always get it right. He watched God do miracle after miracle, from the parting of the Red Sea, to manna falling from the sky, to seeing God pass by him as God hid Moses's face in the crevice of the rock, to God's actual presence being with him. So many miracles (see Exodus 4–16).

Then Moses lost it. He got angry with the people because of their constant complaining of being led into the wilderness. After God told him to speak to the rock so water would flow out of it, Moses disobeyed and struck the rock in anger instead. God provided the water, but Moses' anger cost him ever entering the promised land. To make matters worse, Moses had the gall to take the credit for the miracle rather than naming God as the true source. Anger can make us do stupid stuff (see Numbers 20:1–13). Moses was raised in foster care at an Egyptian palace, became a murderer and a refugee, had a speech impediment, and maybe some anger issues. A true unlikely hero.

Rahab

Rahab had a reputation. To make her not sound so bad, some people like to think of her as an innkeeper, but the plain truth is she was a lady of the night, a prostitute. Yet God chose Rahab as an unlikely hero, not only for the Israelites and her family, but for the whole of humanity. Rahab is the great-great-great-grandmother of King David, placing her in the honored lineage of the Messiah.

God first used Rahab to help the Israelites take the land of Jericho. Joshua sent two spies to check out the land described as flowing with milk and honey. Rahab hid the spies when the king's men came looking for them. Knowing God had given them (the Israelites) the land, she wanted to make sure her family was remembered when everyone else in Jericho was conquered and destroyed. Because of her heroic efforts, the spies were not captured. Her family lived. And a Savior was born (see Joshua 2; Matthew 1:5–16).

David

David is known as a man after God's own heart. Yet, he started out small, the youngest of all of Jesse's sons, a mere boy who tended the sheep back home while his older brothers fought in Saul's army. The teenage shepherd was laughed at when he wanted to fight Goliath the giant. Even Goliath scoffed at the boy coming to fight him. Yet the young David defeated Goliath that day with the Lord's help, a slingshot, and a stone. This definitely got Saul's attention, earning David a spot in the king's service. David went from humble beginnings to the King's detail, only to end up running for his life from Saul's jealousy (see 1 Samuel 17–19).

After Saul's death, David became king, but lustful temptation got the best of him when he saw a beautiful woman bathing. David sent for Bathsheba and got her pregnant. The Bible isn't clear if it was mutual consent. I doubt Bathsheba could have denied the king even if she'd wanted to. David came up with a plan to make it look like her husband got her pregnant, but when Uriah didn't cooperate, David ordered him to the frontlines of battle where Uriah was struck down. David's lust caused him to sin by adultery, possibly rape, and murder. His actions caused the sword to never leave his house. Three of his sons died. His daughter, Tamar, was raped by her stepbrother, and one of David's sons conspired to kill him (see 2 Samuel 11–13; 18).

The mighty warrior David groaned with grief a large part of his adult life. Yet the Bible describes him as a man after God's own heart. My friend, we can learn an important lesson from David.

Although our sin has consequences, God's love never leaves us. He still chooses us, no matter what sins shadow our past. And when we surrender our past sins and current brokenness to Him, when we continue to place our trust in Him, to seek His face, we can become people after God's heart, just like David.

God's Heroes Are Those Who Say Yes to Him

There are so many unlikely heroes, ordinary people, God used in the Bible to lead His people, govern His people, teach His people, love His people, and foretell the greatest message that has ever been told—a Savior was coming who would save His people from their sins. God even used the common, small-town couple Mary and Joseph as heroes to bring up His son, Jesus, here on earth.

In choosing His disciples, Jesus pulled together a band of misfits to share the gospel message. A tax collector. Fishermen. Teenagers. Two of them were called the "Sons of Thunder" (Mark 3:17). Definitely not the elite Hebrew scholars of their day. Ordinary young men, but with a willing spirit to follow, learn, and ultimately start a revolution that changed the world. They said yes to Jesus and became evangelists, preachers, missionaries, and, in the end, martyrs because of their love for Him.

And then there's Paul. Talk about an unlikely candidate for a hero of faith. With a fervent conviction that he was already serving God, Paul hunted down, persecuted, and murdered Christians, trying passionately to snuff out any belief in this "false messiah," as he believed Jesus to be at the time. Until the real Messiah showed up as a bright light and revealed His divine truth to Paul. After Paul encountered the living God, he said yes to what God was truly calling him to do (see Acts 9:1–22).

Paul was some kind of special hero. He understood God's desire to be with us. He felt the same way about God. "For to me, living means living for Christ, and dying is even better. But if I live, I can do more fruitful work for Christ. So I really don't know which is better. I'm torn between two desires: I long to go and be with Christ, which would be far better for me. But for your sakes, it is better that I continue to live" (Philippians 1:21–24). The converted activist launched churches, took missionary journeys, mentored younger missionaries, and spent time in prison. He became one of the most notable apostles, writing nearly half of the New Testament.

Throughout the time of the Bible, God spoke through numerous ordinary heroes to become authors and poets who would listen to the Spirit and write the holy words that would be transcribed into over 3,500 languages[1]. All so that you and I and millions of others would know there is a God who loves us, sees us, and wants a relationship with us.

There was nothing extra special about any of these unlikely heroes of faith. The common denominator was they were willing to say yes to Him when He called.

And here's the good news for you and me. There is a God in heaven who chooses us while we're still broken. We don't have to be cleaned up before we come to Him. He meets us as we are in our brokenness. He builds a message out of our mess and turns our tests into testimonies. God has limitless grace and mercy on tap that He longs to shower upon us. He lovingly, with no judgment or condemnation, invites us into a relationship with Him through His son, Jesus.

There's nothing we've done to earn or deserve this loving relationship with God. It's all because of Him. In His love, He accepts us—in the outward brokenness some of us have and in the inward brokenness we try to hide. That's the good news, my friend. There is hope in our brokenness. Whether our past haunts us, our future terrifies us, or our current situation makes us feel broken beyond repair, Jesus covers it all with His faithfulness, His love, and His longing to walk through the rest of your life with you. It doesn't matter how far away from God or how broken you feel, because of God's promises you are never unloved, you are never unseen, and you are never forgotten. The Creator of all knows you by name and chooses you! The question is, will you choose Him? I hope you say yes.

PRAYER

Dear Jesus, you know everything about me. You know the hidden secrets in my heart. You know the doubts I struggle with and how I've wrestled with believing that you won't accept me because of all my brokenness. I admit that even at this moment I struggle to believe you love me, but Jesus I'm tired, I'm broken, and I can't do it on my own anymore. I want you to come into my heart. Jesus, I know I've screwed up, and I want the guilt and shame to stop screaming in my ear. I believe that you love me, that I need you, that I've sinned and need a Savior. I also believe that you defeated death on the cross and that just like the thief on the cross who said, "Remember me," I, too, can live with you in paradise. Jesus, I place my life and heart into your hands. The old has gone and the new has come. Thank you, Jesus, for loving me and saving me!

In your precious name I pray, Jesus,
Amen.

If you know Jesus but it's time to reignite the fire in your soul, pray this with me.

Dear Jesus, I know that I've been lukewarm lately and that you don't like that. Jesus, give me a heart that cares about what you care about. Help me to be a light in my home, in my career, and in my community. I don't want to just believe in you, Jesus, I want to follow you!

In your precious name I pray, Jesus,
Amen.

TRUE FOR ME

I am God's masterpiece (EPHESIANS 2:10).

Jesus chose me (JOHN 15:16).

God is faithful even if I'm not faithful (2 TIMOTHY 2:13).

I can trust God (PSALM 33:4).

God guards me from evil (2 THESSALONIANS 3:3).

God will forgive my sin and cleanse me (1 JOHN 1:9).

God is my rock (DEUTERONOMY 32:4).

God's Word is trustworthy, encouraging, wholesome, and true
(TITUS 1:9).

Jesus offers me a free gift of eternal life (ROMANS 6:23).

God promises newness for me as His adopted child (ROMANS
8:23).

10

Embrace Your Purpose

I never wanted to go to college. But when I asked my future father-in-law for his blessing to marry his daughter, he asked me how I was going to support her. Before I could answer, he added his advice. "You can't work with your hands long-term. You better get an education."

"Yes sir."

That was the end of the discussion. I didn't have a good argument against what he said, so off to college I went. As newlyweds, Sharla and I attended Northwestern College, a small Christian college just down the road from where we lived. Sharla was studying to be an elementary teacher, and I was just hoping to graduate as soon as I could. My major wasn't that important to me; how quickly I could it get it done was what motivated me the most. I chose to major in business because it seemed the fastest track to graduation.

That was all going smoothly until my Bible classes. I had never dug into the Bible like that before. I was finding hope and redemption and forgiveness as we studied chapter after chapter.

The Bible became so real to me. God became real to me as well. I found myself experiencing a new enthusiasm in my faith; out with the old, in with the new. I understood what the apostle Paul meant when he said, "anyone who belongs to Christ has become a new person. The old life is gone; a new life has begun!" (2 Corinthians 5:17).

I started hearing God's voice in a new way. Most of it felt exhilarating, but some of what I started to hear I didn't like so much. I tried to ignore it, suppress it, make it go away. I sensed Him saying, "Rob, go tell your story."

God, I don't want to tell my story. I don't want to announce to everyone how I failed, how I messed up.

The Spirit began to work inside me. God was calling me to start a nonprofit ministry, but I kept resisting. I didn't know anything about starting a ministry, and I really didn't want to tell people about my story of being angry with God and all the decisions I made that I wasn't proud of. Plus, I didn't want to run a ministry. . . . I wanted to be a farmer, or a banker to help farmers.

"Rob, go tell your story."

God, I can't do that. I can't!

I duked it out with God over what I felt He was calling me to for at least a year, if not longer. I'm not sure what I was waiting for—the healing of my brokenness or for my wife to agree to this crazy life. It finally got to the point where I could no longer say no. God was calling me to share my brokenness, even though I had no idea what it would all look like. I just knew I wouldn't find any peace until I obeyed God's call.

So RISE Ministries began as a way for me to speak out about my own broken story and my personal challenges facing muscular dystrophy. I started telling my story at youth groups, schools, churches, wherever they would let me share. I wanted to help teenagers not make the stupid, dumb mistakes I had made.

Before long, God brought a team of people to work with me in ministry. We kept looking for new ways of encouraging our audience, mostly teens and young adults in the beginning, to help them overcome adversity. After several brainstorming sessions, we came up with an acronym for RISE: Realize, Investigate, Surrender, Enjoy. That became our message of hope. Realize who you are, who God made you to be. Investigate your gifts as well as your weaknesses. Surrender what you can't change. Enjoy a life filled with the hope and joy that can only come through Jesus.

The first six months were tough. The next year and a half didn't get much better. It took more than a year for our local radio manager to take me seriously. We eventually launched a radio program called *Rise Above Radio* that aired locally at the time. The program included segments like short devotionals and "Food for Thought." These brief segments were designed to connect with our listeners regarding relevant issues in their lives, to give them something to think about, hopefully to encourage and inspire them. Interestingly, back in 2010, the theme of one of our "Food for Thought" segments was all about brokenness. Here is a clip from the actual script:

"It seems that broken is a state of where things are at in a lot of people's lives. Beat down, hurt, confused, struggling to make it through. . . . Friend, you may be knocked down, but you're not out forever. God still loves you. God still has a plan for you. God still cares about you. Rise above and get back up again."

Sound familiar? Brokenness continues to be a persistent theme in so many of our lives. The same encouragement we offered our listeners all those years ago applies to you today, my friend.

In those early years of ministry, we created a short-lived magazine called *IMPACT* for teens. The quarterly magazine featured interviews with artists and extreme athletes who had achieved amazing things despite great personal challenges. Then, sooner than anticipated, we ended up canceling *IMPACT* after we realized teenagers didn't read magazines anymore.

After I visited the LifeLight music festival in Sioux Falls, South Dakota, in 2004, at the suggestion of one of our board members,

RISE Ministries took on a new role. In the summer of 2005, our new friends at LifeLight helped us put on our first Christian music festival, Rise Above Fest, in Orange City, Iowa. We offered people a chance to gather and listen to live performances of contemporary Christian music from Jeff Deyo, Shane & Shane, and others. And the people came! We estimated 1,500 to 2,000 in attendance that first year. The next year we presented the festival on our own and changed the name. The music festival known as RiseFest had been born.

I learned a valuable lesson throughout this process: if you think you need to have everything figured out before you share your brokenness with others, you'll never start. If I had believed I needed to have my act together before sharing my story with those teenagers all those years ago, I'd still be waiting. And God for sure knows I would have never listened to the idea of launching a live outdoor Christian music festival. But because I want to obey God and walk closely with Him no matter what, live outdoor Christian music festivals are now very much my thing. So much so, in fact, that I get to serve as chairman of the board for the Christian Festival Association, the national organization that supports two dozen festivals similar to RiseFest across the United States. Trust me, I would have never figured that out on my own.

Just like me, you don't need to have everything figured out before you share your brokenness with others. You never know what God may have in store for you, what blessings and healing are earmarked for you. And none of us knows how God is going to work through our brokenness, whose lives He is going to touch, whose hearts He is going to reach, all because you and I are obedient to His call, whatever that may be. I doubt God will call you to launch a live outdoor Christian music festival like He did me, but He might. More likely, however, He is already stirring your heart with a message of hope. Maybe a nudge of just that one step forward. Meet a new neighbor? Take a new job?

Volunteer for a position at church or a local charity? Write a book? Start a podcast? I challenge you to take that first step. Be brave, my friend. You never know what miracles God will call you to be a part of.

Miracles Happen When We Don't Quit

The recession in 2008 hit us hard at RISE Ministries, as it did many other nonprofits across the nation. The national economy was in the tank, and donors everywhere were pulling back on contributions. We managed the best we could, but eventually the ministry was upside down financially. At one point we had to let the entire staff go, and I took a pay cut. Due to our financial situation, we had many tough discussions in our leadership meetings.

The main debate was over the large amount of money spent on bands and on one weekend every summer. We kept coming back to the question, "Can't that money be used in better ways?"

I guess there was only one way to find out, so we decided not to host the festival that year. That was 2010. I didn't like the decision, but I didn't know what else to do. When we canceled the festival that year, I didn't know if we would ever host another one. I didn't even know what our organization would look like going forward. I tried to take the route I was advised to, but I felt like I was banging my head against the wall.

I became so discouraged, it got to the point I wondered how or if I was going to be able to provide for my family. My father-in-law wouldn't like that, education or not. I was at an all-time low, exhausted, beaten down, and without much hope. Time to have a serious talk with Sharla.

Did I mention my wife was initially against me starting this thing called RISE? She didn't want me spending my life asking people for money. Of course, she quickly recognized how God was leading and jumped in with both feet (it only took eight years).

But now, I wondered what she would say when I told her what I was thinking.

"Sharla, I'm done. I can't do it anymore."

My beautiful wife, who didn't want me to start the ministry in the first place, looked at me and said, "You can't quit now."

"What? I thought you'd be happy with my decision."

Then the wisest words came out of her mouth. "You can't quit unless God tells you to quit, and I don't see that He's doing that. Besides, our kids will have experiences through this ministry that don't happen for everyone."

And my sweet wife has been so right. Jager, Riley, and Aidan have grown up with the ministry. I love watching them serve and bring their friends into the mix as everyone pitches in. As of this writing, Jager oversees the 224 campsites at our festival each summer and travels with me throughout the year, Riley helps emcee, and Aidan is one of our best promoters, running merch and slides. But in those tough years, I was so close to throwing in the towel multiple times. Quitting seemed like a much easier option. Yet every time I was about to, God would provide a glimmer of hope.

Around that time, Jager, at age seven, went with me to a Life-Light concert in my old stomping grounds of Worthington, Minnesota, where I had spent the first years of high school. Brian "Head" Welch, a guitarist and vocalist who had been with the band Korn, was playing that night. He gave his testimony, sharing how he walked away from a 26-million-dollar contract after he found the Lord and how he never looked back.

At the end of the event, Jager and I were leaving the parking lot when he asked from the backseat, "Dad, what was that about tonight?"

"Well, they were praising Jesus. They were having church."

"They were having church?"

"Yeah, they were having church in a gymnasium."

"Dad, that ain't nothin' like the church we go to."

"Nope. No, it's not, son."

He thought about it for a minute. In the rearview mirror, I could see him light up as he thought of something.

"Oh! It's more like your festival!"

I smiled. "Yep, it's more like our festival."

As we drove out onto the road toward home, Jager asked, "Are you doing your festival?"

"No, we're not."

"How come?"

"Because I don't have enough money."

"Dad, is it just your money?"

"No, bud."

"You pull everybody's money together?"

"Yep, we do."

"And you still don't have enough money?"

"No, we don't."

Then, my wise boy shook me to the core with his next words.

"Dad, I'll give you all of my money if you'll bring the festival back."

I had been running so hard for that first decade I didn't realize what the ministry was doing in my own family—I didn't realize it was already blessing my family in ways I never understood.

You know what happened that year of canceling RiseFest? The money didn't come in.

You know what we learned? People like to give to the festival.

We thought we could use the money in better places instead of spending it on the festival, but the problem is that without the festival, the money wasn't there.

I sat down and said to my leadership team, "I don't ever want to have this conversation again on whether the festival is valuable. We just need to figure out a way to do it."

The next year, 2011, we brought the festival back in a very small way. Then my local community came calling in 2012, and it's been the craziest ride ever since.

A generous corporation saw our need for permanent grounds. We had been leasing the property with the understanding it could be pulled from us within twenty-four to forty-eight hours if a big business came in and wanted that piece of land. We ran on faith for five years, believing that would never happen. What a blessing (and relief) when the corporation bought the first half of the grounds on our behalf in 2018. A couple of years later they bought the second half of the grounds. So now all the land is privately owned on behalf of RISE Ministries and RiseFest. We have permanent buildings on the grounds that have been donated by generous donors. In 2020 (the only other year we canceled the festival, this time due to Covid), we were able to build a permanent stage called the Harvest Stage.

RISE Ministries has always been about more than the festival. We have hosted mission trips, podcasts, TV broadcasts, "Stories of Strength" videos, "Rise with Rob & Friends Night Out," and more. We also partner with other ministries to reach more broken people, like Touch of Hope Haiti, working to strengthen families in Haiti through education, orphan care, and job creation. They have a small building on our permanent grounds that is a replica of their building in Simonette, Haiti, where festival goers can purchase Haitian goods to help meet the mission of strengthening families in Haiti.

Since the day we started RISE, our budget has grown well over nineteen times. The RiseFest Christian music festival has become one of the largest of its kind and is ever growing. Every year we hear stories from attendees telling us how much the weekend means to them. Viewers and listeners of our broadcasts send in similar reports. People's lives are being renewed in Jesus as they worship at the festival and learn at the seminars as well as in our online ministries. Considering how I had no idea what I was doing, I'd say all of this is evidence of a miracle-working God pulling His people together for His purpose.

It's mind-boggling to consider all the blessings we would have missed if I had quit during the hard times. And the same is true for you! Trust Him and press on to whatever, wherever, God is calling you to. Be open to however He wants you to share in your brokenness for the benefit of others. Maybe He simply is asking you to share your story.

There is power in our stories. Sharing your story might be one of the hardest things you ever do. That's possible. But the opposite is possible as well—it might be the easiest way to receive the healing you need. I've been able to share this story of brokenness for decades, and I tell people all the time it's part of the healing process for me. Every time I get to talk about the hard things or laugh at the awkward things, I find a little peace I didn't have before. Only God knows what is on the other side of our obedience.

Shining the Light of Jesus into Dark Brokenness

God knew there was another reason I couldn't quit, a reason that still makes my blood boil as I think about it. There is a noble, necessary goal we are determined to achieve at RiseFest, and I hope you will join us. I am asking as many of us as possible to gather together to make a statement, to replace an unspeakable wrong, to show that God loves all people, every variety and in every kind of brokenness. Let me explain.

The attendance to our annual RiseFest has continued to increase over the years. In a rural town of 5,500 or so, it has been nothing less than amazing to see so many people travel to our location from around the country. When attendance hit 20,000, I was convinced the gatherings at our Christian music festivals were the biggest crowds our little Iowa town had ever seen—until someone told me about the Ku Klux Klan gathering in Sheldon around one hundred years ago. That gathering was bigger than RiseFest, they said. Surely they were misinformed. I found that sickening claim hard to believe, so I went to the museum and saw the actual display for myself. I was shocked at what I saw.

On June 21, 1924, a "Konklave" or "Kall of the Klan" was held at the Sheldon Fairgrounds on the west edge of town. An estimated twenty-five thousand members from all over Iowa were in attendance, awarding the Ku Klux Klan the record of hosting the largest gathering on record for Sheldon[1]. Twenty-five thousand! Thousands and thousands of stupid hooded Klan members in our small town. That was just plain wrong.

And they made a day of it. The guys played baseball (probably not wearing their pointy hats, but who knows?), gave speeches, and listened to bands perform. They had concession stands and booths where they sold Klan swag like literature and songbooks. If you paid your dues of twenty-four dollars, they'd throw in the robe and hood along with it. Kind of sounds like a live outdoor music festival, doesn't it? Creeps me out to think about it.

My first thought was, *That sucks.* Stupid KKK was the largest gathering in Sheldon after all, not RiseFest. Then it became clear to me: We need to beat that record. For so many reasons.

The KKK declared themselves the boss of religion and morality in America. They gave money to charities and churches, and members ran for public office so they could have more influence. That day at the museum, I learned that the Klan was anti-foreign, anti-Catholic, anti-Jewish, anti-Black, anti-pacifist, anti-Communist, anti-bootlegger, and anti–birth control. If anyone fit into one of those categories and crossed the KKK line, they could be whipped, tarred, and feathered. It's hard to imagine.

The thing that hit me most is that the KKK movement was all about what and who it was *against*. Klansmen were against people who were different. They were against people who didn't look like them, against people who didn't think the same as them. At RISE, instead of being about something we're against, we're about something we're *for*. Our gathering, RiseFest, is for people, all people. We are for glorifying God. We're for worshiping together as a community. We. Are. For. And the main focus of what we're for is telling people about Jesus and letting people understand there's a God who loves them. It became my goal to blot out this dark spot in the history books by replacing the KKK's record with a far more worthy gathering.

When RiseFest attendance hit twenty thousand in 2022, it became real. We will beat this dark record! June of 2024 marks the one-hundredth anniversary of perhaps the darkest spot in Sheldon's history. Every year going forward, as more and more of us gather at RiseFest each summer, the light of God's goodness will continue to overshadow the evil of the KKK's oppression. As soon as more than twenty-five thousand people attend RiseFest to worship the God of hope instead of gathering for hate, we will officially replace the one-hundred-year-old dark record with a new one. A new record that shines God's love, not hate. And His light will go with us back to our homes, to our communities, to the world, defeating the darkness everywhere we go. Because "the Spirit who lives in you is greater than the spirit who lives in the world" (1 John 4:4).

There is way too much dark brokenness in this world as a result of the Enemy's influence. As Christians, we are to shine the light of Jesus into those dark places. "'In the same way, let your light shine before others, that they may see your good deeds and glorify your Father in heaven'" (Matthew 5:16 NIV). Think of all the other broken people who are living in darkness, without the hope of Jesus. What a difference it could make in their lives if we reached out in the name of Jesus with a loving hand, to show concern, give a listening ear. Where is Jesus calling you to shine His light? I also choose to continually ask myself, *Where is He calling me?* Let's go ahead and be like the scrappy disciples following after Jesus, sometimes clumsy and not always doing it right, but passionate all the same. *God, show us how we can replace the dark brokenness in this world with your shining light and with your healing love!*

After Jesus rose from the dead, He had a secret rendezvous with the disciples (minus Judas) on a mountain in Galilee. He told them, "'I have been given all authority in heaven and on earth. Therefore, go and make disciples of all the nations, baptizing them in the name of the Father and the Son and the Holy Spirit. Teach these new disciples to obey all the commands I have given you. And be sure of this: I am with you always, even to the end of the age'" (Matthew 28:18–20). Jesus knew His guys well. He knew they still had doubts, fears, tempers, arguments. He knew they still had brokenness that doesn't heal overnight. Yet He called them to go in His name. He calls us to do the same, to go and share His good news. And He doesn't leave us to do it on our own—He promises to be with us "always, even to the end of the age."

With God's help, we can make a difference in this broken world. Not so much by being strong, perfect followers of Jesus, because . . . well, we've covered that ground. It's not about us at all, is it? It's about walking in step with the Holy Spirit, renewing our minds with God's truth, letting Jesus shine through us, our brokenness and all. Brokenness doesn't disqualify any of us from being a tool in God's hand. It's about whether we allow God to use us in our brokenness.

God Comforts Us So We Can Comfort Others

God's faithfulness has been and continues to be prevalent on this journey of mine. I have watched His hand open doors when I thought they were locked for good. When Sharla and I thought there was no way we could build a house with the necessary accessibility for me, God's faithfulness proved me wrong, providing for our needs once again. In the challenging times, He has been faithful, from the small details to the big details. That faithfulness is for all of His followers. That means you too.

My friend, I hope you're feeling God's comfort. Knowing He sees you, loves you, and knows you by name. Your brokenness doesn't keep you from God; it can actually bring you closer to

Him. This is the comfort I've received from Him, and I want you to have it as well.

The same comfort we have received from God is the comfort He calls us to share with others. My good pal Paul the apostle understood this well. In fact, he lays it out better than I could. "He comforts us in all our troubles so that we can comfort others. When they are troubled, we will be able to give them the same comfort God has given us. For the more we suffer for Christ, the more God will shower us with his comfort through Christ. Even when we are weighed down with troubles, it is for your comfort and salvation! For when we ourselves are comforted, we will certainly comfort you. Then you can patiently endure the same things we suffer" (2 Corinthians 1:4–6).

I'm broken both outwardly and inwardly, yet God loves me. Just like He loves you right where you are. I don't have all the answers, but I believe in a God who does. Still one of the hardest truths for me to embrace is knowing that Almighty God can heal me at any moment, and that at this time He has chosen not to. I've wrestled with that paradox for years, and I know I'm not alone. I've heard it shared by the likes of Bart Millard of MercyMe whose son has dealt with chronic diabetes since age two. It's a tough question with no clear answer. Why do some get healed while others don't?

God brought a new friend, Shaila, into my life to help me come to peace with this mystery. As a guest on our podcast, Shaila shared the story of a dear friend of hers—a wife, mother, and friend—who was recently diagnosed with cancer. They prayed for miraculous healing, but her friend lost her battle and went on to be with Jesus. Then, out of nowhere, Shaila was diagnosed with a rare disease. Healing didn't seem possible, but through prayer she was miraculously healed. She shared on the podcast the question that nagged at her. "God, why was I healed when my friend, a wife and mother, wasn't?"

After sitting in prayer and seeking God with this question, she arrived at a place of comfort. When asked how she dealt with it all, her answer penetrated my heart. I listened even more carefully as she continued.

"Somehow in the midst of this, I can hold in one hand disappointment, grief, longing for a different result, and in the other hand, joy at the power of a miraculous God who can do anything. And so, I love praying for healing for people, and I pray with deep faith, because I've experienced it myself, but I don't pray in a way that doesn't honor disappointment, grief, sadness, and a real longing for miracles that don't happen."

Purpose in the pain. Acceptance of a harsh reality while at the same time trusting in the comfort of God's sovereignty. So far, the miracle of physical healing hasn't happened in my life, and at times it's hard. I long for healing. I want my independence back or just the simple privilege of walking. Yet I continue on because in the midst of the hardships, God comforts me. He reminds me that He sees me, He loves who I am, He has never and will never, ever, ever forget me. And He is using me in my disappointment, my grief, and my sadness in ways that would never have happened if I hadn't chosen to live my life in His will.

My friend, no matter what your life looks like right now—broken, healed, recovering, or somewhere in between—God still chooses you. We have all been dealt a dose of brokenness at one time or another in varying ways. And if we can be transparent with one another, we'd have to admit we've each had our own wrestling matches with God. Jacob, who later became Israel, wrestled with God all night and ended up with a limp for the rest of his life, but he got his blessing. If you're like me, you may have been in a lock hold much longer than one night. I feel like I have wrestled with God for years. All right, I confess; I still tend to take Him to the mat now and then. But in the end, He always proves His goodness.

When you seek the face of Jesus above all other options, your eyes will be opened to how much He loves you and wants the best for you. Even the grieving David would agree. "Hear my voice when I call, LORD; be merciful to me and answer me. My heart says of you, 'Seek his face!' Your face, LORD, I will seek" (Psalm 27:7–8 NIV). In his brokenness, David knew he could still trust in God's goodness. "I remain confident of this: I will see the goodness of the LORD in the land of the living" (Psalms 27:13 NIV). In our current land of the living, it seems the Enemy is running rampant these days. It's not always easy to see the goodness of the Lord. That doesn't mean it isn't there. Our modern culture tries to convince us to believe lies and take on labels from the Enemy, and if we get spiritually careless or try to handle our brokenness on our own, we leave ourselves vulnerable. But when we earnestly seek His face, God's relentless love exposes the lies and replaces the false labels with His true ones: loved, seen, chosen.

God works in and through our weakness to show His strength, and we don't need to take everything so doggone seriously. We learn the healing power of grieving and the comfort that comes from entering into one another's broken journeys. Our brokenness takes on a greater purpose when we share it with others. I hope you have seen that Jesus is here for you. Not a single one of us is unloved, unseen, or forgotten by Him.

PRAYER

Dear Jesus, thank you for loving me so deeply and reminding me that I am loved, seen, and remembered. I know that your Word tells me that you know how many hairs or lack thereof are on my head. Help me to believe it and hold onto this truth the next time life gets hard and I begin to question your love for me. Let that love of yours flow out of me so that I may be an instrument you use to shine in dark places. Give me to the courage to continue on in faith until the day you take me home.

I love you, Jesus,
Amen.

TRUE FOR ME

Jesus tells me all things are possible with Him (MARK 10:27).

God created me wonderfully complex (PSALM 139:14).

Jesus can work miracles for me (LUKE 9:16–17).

The Holy Spirit fills me with boldness (ACTS 4:31).

God will restore, support, and strengthen me (1 PETER 5:10).

God reminds me nothing is too hard for Him (JEREMIAH 32:27).

God gives me peace beyond comprehension (PHILIPPIANS 4:6–7).

God is with me in difficult times (ISAIAH 43:2).

God has greater purpose in my troubles (JAMES 1:2–4).

I help others when I stand strong in my faith (JOSHUA 24:14–16).

Jesus is with me as I share His truth (MATTHEW 28:19–20).

ACKNOWLEDGMENTS

So many incredible people have been a part of this journey. Without each one of you, I wouldn't have learned the lessons or experienced the stories I get to share. It's been quite the ride!

To my wife, Sharla: From the first time I saw you walk into that library in high school, to finally asking you out on a very long phone call, you've shown me the love of Christ, and my life has never been the same. It was through you that I experienced what loving someone with no strings attached looks like. This book happened because of your love, support, and belief in me. I'm so grateful for you!

To our kids: Jager—our first born. My son. I wasn't sure what raising a boy would be like, being a dad with limited mobility. I worried that you'd resent me or be angry that your dad couldn't do certain things. And yet, now that you've grown into a young man, I couldn't have been more wrong. You are loving, caring, and helpful. You've blessed me with so many memories of traveling with me (since you were two years old), going to football games, concerts, and coming alongside me and the ministry of RISE where and when you can. Riley—my sweet, redheaded, feisty daughter. You are a strong, passionate young lady. And you have a compassionate love for those who are considered "different." It melts my heart to watch you care for and love people who so often feel unloved, unseen, and forgotten. Aidan—your spirit is so sweet, and your personality is one of a kind. You bring laughter and wit to situations that just make life better. Your heart is kind, and you care deeply for others. I know because I get to be one of the ones you care for. Kids, I couldn't be happier to be your dad. Our life hasn't looked like others', but you've always been up for the adventure. You've stepped in to help when the need arose. You've learned to care for others and see needs without being asked, and each of your hearts radiates love.

To my family: Dad, your constant example of following and loving Jesus has helped me more than I can say. I know I tease you a lot about your career change in your mid-thirties, but it was what God had in store for our family. Through adversity, challenges, and hardships, you've remained faithful, and it hasn't been unnoticed. Thank you for loving Jesus the way you do! Mom, Amy, and Bill, I know this journey of MD has not always been easy for you to experience with me. At times the journey was extremely difficult, and I didn't always treat you well. Thanks for not giving up on me.

To my extended family who has blessed me in so many ways: Ed and Shirley, Steve and Sheila, Dave and Shelly, Shane and Christie, and all the wonderful nephews and nieces I got through this amazing family. The "We'll do whatever it takes" attitude has blessed me in so many ways over the years and has allowed me to experience dreams I've longed to accomplished. Thank you for your generous hearts and servant attitudes.

To our RISE and RiseFest team and board: Jarrett, Kory and Julie, Eddie G., Bobbi and Micaela, Kolton, Jack and Tina, Jerry and Kim, Ken, Allison, Caitie, Rachael, Piet, Dominic, Troy, Jen, Leah, Jesse, Tim and Kelli, Molly, Sarah, Erica, Eddie V., Jamie, Jay and Alicia, Jon, Dan, Hannah, Kandi, Kaleigh, Rodolfo, Monty, Laurie, Scott, Tricia, and Melany. This work would not be possible without all of you believing in loving and serving others like Jesus. It is amazing what God does through all your tireless hours of pointing people to Jesus. My heart is extremely blessed!

To Ellie, our creative brain: If it wasn't for you, this title wouldn't exist. Your gifts and talents for creating are such a blessing. The crazy ideas I sometimes come up with, you put into play and make happen. Thank you for believing in telling stories of how God meets us in our pain and never leaves us whether we're on the mountaintop or in the depths of the valley.

To my TLP Crew: Matt, Kree, Amy, Alex, and Shannon. If it wasn't for your nudge and push to encourage me to write, I would've never gotten this far. I love the journey we've been on together.

To Jay, my friend who has taught me "It'll be fine," to "include others, serve well, and be generous," and so many other great lessons in life. The adventures have been unbelievable; some of them are shared throughout these pages. Your and Alicia's encouragement pushes me day-in and day-out to continue the journey God has called me to, and I'm so glad you're on it with me and my family!

To Chad, Maria, and Caleb: You are so dear to me. I can't thank you enough for letting me share your and Tripp's story. Your son and brother have touched me in ways I can't explain, and your faith through extreme grief has continued to point me to Jesus as I navigate my own!

To Chris McFarland: You saw the potential of this book and put the pieces in motion to introduce me to the right people to get it done. Thank you for believing.

To Kathy Groom, my friend and writer: I never thought I'd write a book because I really didn't enjoy writing, and to be honest, I have been told I can't write. But you made this process not be so hard, and I actually enjoyed it! I appreciate your tireless work of editing, writing, and rewriting on this message that I've been wanting to get out for so long. Your encouragement and passion to help me get the words down on paper mean so much to me. Thank you. This book wouldn't be what it is without you.

To David Sluka, Hope Johnson, Bethany Lenderink, and the Baker team: David, thank you for going the extra mile to help bring out the message that was living inside of me and pushing it on the fast track to get it out there sooner than later. Hope and Bethany, thank you for your fresh insight to point out how to make this book even better. And thank you to the entire team who each played an important role in getting this book published so quickly.

And finally, to all our partners and friends at RISE Ministries. Thank you, thank you, thank you for believing in the vision to reach and inspire every community through the transforming hope in Jesus. My heart is so overwhelmed at your generosity to help point as many people as we can to Jesus! He is what RISE Ministries and this book are all about.

NOTES

Chapter 1 Everyone Is Broken

1. Mayo Clinic Staff, "Muscular dystrophy," Mayo Clinic, February 11, 2022, https://www.mayoclinic.org/diseases-conditions/muscular-dystrophy/symptoms-causes/syc-20375388.

2. Thomas Lake, "Did This Man Really Cut Michael Jordan?" *Sports Illustrated* Vault, January 16, 2012, https://vault.si.com/vault/2012/01/16/did-this-man-really-cut-michael-jordan.

Chapter 4 Labels Hurt

1. 2 Samuel 9, 19:24–30, 21:7

2. *Oxford Advanced Learner's Dictionary*, s.v. "set apart (*phrasal verb*)," accessed October 30, 2023, https://www.oxfordlearnersdictionaries.com/us/definition/english/set-apart.

Chapter 5 Learning to Grieve so We Can Heal

1. John Townsend (@drjohntownsend), "Grief is a sign that someone mattered, and grief in community is cut in half. Don't isolate. Remember that social-distancing doesn't mean social-isolation," Twitter, April 8, 2020, https://twitter.com/drjohntownsend/status/1248004208978059265.

Chapter 6 Weakness Shows Strength

1. *Merriam-Webster*, s.v. "sacrifice (v.)," accessed October 25, 2023, https://www.merriam-webster.com/dictionary/sacrifice.

Chapter 9 God Still Chooses You

1. "2023 Global Scripture Access," Wycliffe Global Alliance, accessed October 26, 2023, https://www.wycliffe.net/resources/statistics/.

Chapter 10 Embrace Your Purpose

1. Sheldon Historical Society, "The KKK in Iowa in the 1920s," *Prairie Queen Annual Newsletter*, no. 39 (2012): pp. 4–11.

Rob Roozeboom is passionate about helping people find hope! He's the founder and president of RISE Ministries, Inc. in Sheldon, Iowa. Rob didn't let a muscular dystrophy diagnosis at age five slow his ambitions. By 2005, he and team members launched RiseFest through RISE Ministries, a Christian Music Festival that now lives in Sheldon and hosts about twenty thousand people over two days. Rob also hosts a podcast called *Enjoying the Journey* and has interviewed pro athletes, authors, psychologists, evangelists, pastors, and more to share their real-life stories of overcoming adversity through Jesus. Rob and the team produce an online videos series entitled *Stories of Strength* and have produced Christmas and Good Friday TV broadcasts now reaching thousands. Rob is sought out to share his story and bring Jesus' message of hope to communities, businesses, and prominent events nationwide.

In 2001 and 2002, Rob was featured on the National Jerry Lewis MDA Telethon, was named a Goodwill Ambassador for the state of Iowa in 2005, and was named a Service to HumanKind Award recipient by Northwestern College in 2008. He now sits on the Christian Festival Association (CFA) board, continues to grow RiseFest and RISE Ministries, and delivers his message of hope nationwide. Rob currently lives in Sheldon with his wife, Sharla, a kindergarten teacher, and three kids, their son, Jager (21), and daughters, Riley (18), and Aidan (16).